FOLLOWING GOD THROUGH THE AGES

Your life is a journey you must travel with a deep consciousness of God.

Al Weesner

By

ALVIN O. WEESNER

DEDICATION

This book is dedicated to my Pastors, Paul and Denise Goulet, senior pastors of the International Church of Las Vegas in Las Vegas, Nevada.

I arrived at their church in a wheelchair, broken in body, emotionally distraught and suffering with trauma.   Through the years they have ministered to me, and through the atmosphere of intense worship, love and godly fellowship, I have been restored to awesome health in spirit, soul and body.

TABLE OF CONTENTS

INTRODUCTION

HOW GOD DEALS WITH PEOPLE

Israel under the Law
The Levitic Covenant
The Palestinian Covenant
The Salt Covenant
The Davidic Covenant
Relationship of Law and Grace

INTRODUCTION

God has always existed since He is an eternal being. In the dateless past, God created the universe with millions of galaxies. Earth is a small planet in the Milky Way Galaxy.

There are trillions of solar systems beyond ours. In this study, we will just concern ourselves with some of the facts about our solar system. I want you to grasp and understand how large and powerful our God is, by understanding some of what He has created.

The sun is about 93 million miles from the earth. It is 865,400 miles in diameter, weighs about 1,980 septillion tons, and is considered a dwarf star compared to others. It is 1.3 million times bigger than the earth and 300,000 times closer to us than any other fixed star. It is a large magnet, as are all fixed stars and planets, and is the center of our solar system of 9 major planets, 31 known satellites, and innumerable asteroids and meteors. The temperature of the sun is 12,000 degrees on its surface and 40 million degrees at its center.

Flames shoot up from its surface from 25,000 to 500,000 miles.

The sun rotates on its axis, making a complete turn in about 25 days, and a circuit of the entire heavens once each year in conjunction with all other fixed stars or suns, which move through space at a speed of 12 miles a second or 43,200 MPH. The movement of these is at such a vast distance from us that they appear to be almost at rest. The sun goes forth as a bridegroom and as a strongman, to run a race from one part of heaven to the other (Psalm 19:1-6), the rapid speed being 43,200 MPH. Its family of major planets turn on their own axes, and all revolve around the sun at various distances, as follows:

1. MERCURY, 3,000 miles in diameter, revolves nearest to the sun in a 36 million mile orbit in 85 days.
2. VENUS, 7,600 miles in diameter, is the second nearest the sun, and travels in its 67.2 million mile orbit in 275 days.
3. EARTH, 7,927 miles in diameter, is the third nearest the sun, and travels in its 92.9 million miles orbit in 365.25 days.
4. MARS, 4,200 miles in diameter, is fourth from the sun, and travels in its orbit of 141.5 million miles in 687 days.
5. JUPITER, 88,700 miles in diameter, is fifth, and travels in its 483.3 million mile orbit in almost 12 years.
6. SATURN, 75,100 miles in diameter, is sixth from the sun, and travels in its 886.1 mile orbit in 29.5 years.

7. URANUS, 30,900 miles in diameter, travels in the seventh orbit of 1, 783 million miles in 84 years.
8. NEPTUNE, 27,700 miles in diameter, travels in the eighth orbit of 2,793 million miles in about 165 years.
9. PLUTO, 3,600 miles in diameter, travels in its 3,666 million mile orbit in about 284.5 years.

The last three planets named have been discovered in somewhat recent times: Uranus was discovered in 1781; Neptune was discovered in 1846; and Pluto was discovered in 1930. All the planets but these three appear to the naked eye as bright stars. Uranus is faint; Neptune, fainter to the eye: Pluto is so faint that it was only discovered by long exposure photographs with a powerful telescope.

The 31 known satellites are moons. The Earth has 1 moon; Mars, 2; Jupiter, 12: Saturn, 9; Uranus,5; and Neptune, 2.. A number of other moons or satellites which are very faint, have been discovered only in recent years. Asteroids or minor planets within the range of telescopes, number many thousands. Only 2,000 have been photographed and no more than 1,600 have been observed sufficiently to determine their orbits with fair accuracy. Each year, about 100 more minor planets are detected, but only a score are followed to determine their orbits.

Many comets have been seen. A dozen or so are picked up each year, but relatively few return to visibility in 1,000 years. Their orbits are very elongated, and they can be seen only a short time when they are near the sun. Most of them travel beyond the distant planets, and therefore, cannot be seen. Halley's comet travels about 3.2 million miles away from the sun.

Meteors are seen only when they rush into the atmosphere of the earth and burn up. They are the small shooting stars often seen at night. The air friction heats meteors to about 4,000 degrees. They are first seen about 80 miles above the earth, then burn up between 30 to 40 miles above it.

Distances out in space are measured by light-years. How far light travels in a year at the rate of 186,324 miles a second (speed of light), or about 5.8 trillion miles, is recognized as one light-year. It takes light 400 years to reach earth from the North Star; 700,000 years for it to reach us from the Great Nebula, the galaxy nearest our own; and 500 million years for light to reach us from the faintest galaxy seen by our telescopes.

Gravitation is the power that holds all these heavenly bodies in their own orbits in space. They orbit eternally with unerring precision so that man can accurately foretell, hundreds of years in advance, their location in the heavens, and the exact hour, minute and second, when eclipses will take place.

Some people believe this all just happened without a supernatural designer! The sky proves the existence of God!

The earth and all planets are round (Psalm 19:1-6; Isaiah 40:22). The earth turns on its own axis eastward at more than 1,000 MPH. Each year the earth revolves more than 584 million miles around the sun, at the rate of 66,700 MPH or 1.6 million miles a day. The earth's revolution round the sun establishes our year; its rotation on its axis establishes our day. The 23.5 degree inclination of the earth's axis and its journey around the sun cause the change of seasons and varying lengths of night and day. The earth requires 365 days, 5 hours, 48 minutes, and 46 seconds to complete one revolution around the sun; and 23 hours and 56 minutes to complete one rotation on its axis.

The moon, mentioned 62 times in Scripture, is the earth's satellite, and revolves around the earth. It is a dark, opaque body and the ruler of night (Genesis 1:14-18; Psalm136:9) and seasons (Psalm 104:19). The half turned toward the sun is always bright and the other half, unilluminated, is therefore not visible. While the moon is going once completely around the earth, different regions of the illuminated half are turned toward us, causing the different phases of the moon.

Just as the sun has a north and south motion in a period of a year, so the moon has a similar motion in a period of a month. It rises about 50 minutes later from day to day in the month's cycle. It travels toward the east among the stars, and makes a complete circle each month. It is the nearest to earth of all celestial bodies, except meteors and an occasional comet, being about 221,000 miles away at the nearest point and 253,000 miles at the farthest point of its monthly cycle.

It is said that there are more than 40 sextillion stars, which are suns to other planets like our sun is to our solar system. Most of them are believed to be larger than our sun. The nearest star to the earth, aside from the sun, is Alpha Centauri, about 4.5 light-years or 26.1 trillion miles from the earth. Others range from this vast distance on into infinite space, beyond what any telescope can reveal. On a clear night, the eye can see about 3,000 stars or suns. There are about 30 billion that astronomers can photograph singly. The multitudes of other stars are so close together they appear as a solid mass to us.

Some stars, as Antares (390 million miles in diameter) and Epsilon Aurigae (2.4 billion million miles in diameter) are giants compared to our sun of only 865,400 miles in diameter. The heaviest known stars are said to weigh 100 times more than our sun which, in turn, weighs 330,000 times more than the earth, which weighs 6 sextillion tons.

The surface temperatures of stars range from 5,000 to 26,000 degrees, and the inner temperature from 100,000 to 30,000,000 degrees F. Stars are supposed to be made up of gasses. At least, all the elements we know would be turned into gases at temperatures which exist on most of the stars. The most conspicuous elements on our sun are hydrogen, calcium, sodium, magnesium and iron. The average density of our sun is much lighter than the earth. Its force of gravity at the surface is about 28 times that of the earth, so that a man weighing 150 lbs. on earth would weigh about 2 tons on the sun.

Now, let's follow God through the ages of dispensations and covenants.

HOW GOD DEALS WITH PEOPLE

The Bible reveals that Christianity is a consistent religion. For many thousands of years, God has dealt with His people in the same way – through covenants. We see God making covenant agreements with people and groups throughout the Bible.

> Adam and Eve (Genesis 2:15-17; Hosea 6:7).
> Noah (Genesis 6:18; 9:9-17)
> Abraham (Genesis 15:18-21)
> The nation of Israel (Exodus 20)
> David and his descendants (2 Samuel 7:4-17)
> God speaks of ending His covenant with rebellious Israel and Judah (Jeremiah 31:31-34; Ezekiel 16:59-63), enabling God to establish a New Covenant with them – and with us – established by Jesus' perfect sacrifice on our behalf (Hebrews 7-10; Luke 22:20; Mark 14:24).

Just as with the older covenants, the new covenant is initiated by God, based on repentance and belief in God's promises, and sealed in blood. At the heart of the New Covenant is the same promise God made to His Old Covenant saints: He pledges to redeem all who place their faith in God's promise to save His people from their sin. God has never failed to keep His promises to any other person or group, and He will not fail to keep His covenant promises to you

CHAPTER I

DISPENSATIONS AND COVENANTS

Ephesians 3:2 (KJV) "If ye have heard of the **dispensation of the grace of God** which is given me to you-ward:"

People must recognize the relationship between a dispensation and a covenant, if they would understand God's plan and objective throughout the ages. A <u>dispensation</u> is an administration within a period of time that is based on a conditional test to determine if people will be faithful to God and His conditions.

The Oxford English Dictionary says that <u>dispensation</u> is "the religious or political system of a particular time." What is a dispensation? The word itself comes from the Greek word, OIKONOMIA, and means administration, stewardship, managing of a household or estate. The word is not found in the Old Testament, but occurs four times in the New Testament, but occurs four times in the New Testament: I Corinthians 9:17, Ephesians 1:10; 3:2; Colossians 1:25.

Dispensationalism is also a method of interpreting history that divides God's work and purposes toward mankind into different periods of time. Usually, there are seven dispensations identified, although some theologians believe there are nine. Others count as few as three or as many as thirty-seven dispensations. However, there are seven basic dispensations found in Scripture.

As used in connection with a study of God's eternal program, it may be defined as a probationary period in man's history when God tests him according to a fixed standard of conduct or responsibility, under which man is expected to remain true.

Of the seven dispensations of God's dealing with man, two came before the Flood in the period spoken of as the Antediluvian Age. This period extended from the re-creation of the earth following its chaotic condition, and the creation of man, to the Flood. The dispensations of Innocence and Conscience occurred in this period.

In the Postdiluvian Age, which began after the Flood and will continue until the Millennium, there have been four dispensations: Human Government, Promise , Law, and Grace. We are in the dispensation of Grace at present.

The dispensation of Divine Government, which begins with Christ's return is considered in the Millennial rather than in the Postdiluvian Age.

A covenant is an eternal agreement made by God with humanity, revealing what God will do for people individually or collectively. God made covenants with the human race throughout history that specifically relate to one of the seven dispensations. Each covenant reveals principles in embryonic form by which God will relate to humanity.

Man can choose to reject the covenant or principles of God, and will, to some extent, in every dispensation. When he violates the covenant, man suffers the consequences in the form of a judgment, bringing that dispensation to an abrupt end. Most all Christians recognize at least two dispensations – Law and Grace.

We must understand the various ways God deals with man if he keeps in mind the great broad aspects of God's plan as revealed in a study of the dispensations.

What a skeleton is to the body, what an outline is to a book, dispensations are to the content of the Bible. They give shape to God's eternal program. They give a knowledge of God, His dealings with man, and His ultimate plan, showing definite order and arrangement.

15 GREAT COVENANTS
OF SCRIPTURE

Solaric Covenant

(Genesis 1:14-18; 8:22; Psalm 89:34-37; Jeremiah 31:35-37; 33:19-26).

The Solaric Covenant was made between God and Man. It promised eternal seasons of fruitfulness and that man would continue forever – as long as the solar system endures. In this connection definite promises were made to Noah, David, and others, as seen in the above scriptures.

Genesis 1:14-18 (NLT) "Then God said, "Let lights appear in the sky to separate the day from the night. Let them mark off the seasons, days, and years. Let these lights in the sky shine down on the earth.' And that is what happened. God made two great lights – the larger one to govern the day, and the smaller one to govern the night. He also made the stars. God set these lights in the sky to light the earth, to govern the day and night, and to separate the light from the darkness. And God saw that it was good."

Genesis 1:28 (KJV) "And God blessed them, and God said unto them, 'Be fruitful, and multiply, and replenish the earth, and subdue it: and have dominion over the fish of the sea, and over the fowl of the air, and over every living thing that moves about upon the earth.'"

Genesis 8:22 (NLT) "As long as the earth remains, there will be planting and harvest, cold and heat, summer and winter, day and night."

Psalm 89:34-37 (NLT) "No, I will not break my covenant, I will not take back a single word I said. I have sworn an oath to David, and in my holiness I cannot lie: His Dynasty will go on forever; his kingdom will endure as the sun. It will be as eternal as the moon, My faithful witness in the sky!"

Jeremiah 31:35-37 (NLT) "It is the Lord who provides the sun to light the day and the moon and stars to light the night, and who stirs the sea into roaring waves. His name is the Lord of Heaven's Armies, and this is what He says: "I am as likely to reject my people Israel as I am to abolish the laws of nature!' This is what the Lord says: 'Just as the heavens cannot be measured and the foundations of the earth cannot be explored, so I will not consider casting them away for the evil they have done. I, the Lord, have spoken!'"

Jeremiah 33:19-26 (NLT) "Then this message came to Jeremiah from the Lord: 'This is what the Lord says: If you can break My covenant with the day and the night so that one does not follow the other, only then will My covenant with My servant David be broken. Only then will he no longer have a descendant to reign on his throne. The same is true for My covenant with the Levitical priests who minister before Me. And as the stars of the sky cannot be counted and the sand on the seashore cannot be measured, so I will multiply the descendants of My servant David and the Levites who minister before Me.'

"The Lord gave another message to Jeremiah. He said, 'Have you noticed what people are saying? – The Lord chose Judah and Israel and then abandoned them!' They are sneering and saying that Israel is not worthy to be counted as a nation. But this is what the Lord says: "I would no more reject My people than I would change My laws that govern night and day, earth and sky. I will never abandon the descendants of Jacob or David, My servant, or change the plan that David's descendants will rule the descendants of Abraham, Isaac, and Jacob. Instead, I will restore them to their land and have mercy on them.'"

This covenant was made between God and man. It promised eternal seasons of fruitfulness and that man would continue forever – as long as the solar system endures. In this connection definite promises were made to Noah, David ,and others as seen in the above scriptures.

CHAPTER II

DISPENSATION OF INNOCENCE
(Genesis 2:7 – 3:21)

Some things are unique about this first dispensation. Into each of the subsequent dispensations man enters with a sinful record of failure. But Adam and Eve came fresh from the hand of God, endowed with all that was pure and good, with no past, and with the most perfect future within their grasp.

They had perfect physical life, with no inherited weaknesses or tendencies that would cast a shadow over their lives together. They had daily communion with the God Who created them. He actually "came down" and talked with them every evening.

They had satisfying work to do in an unblemished world. Adam needed no books or formal education to be able to name the animals. He simply knew their names by intuition. He could draw upon God's infinite knowledge through communion with Him.

Having such physical and spiritual likeness to the God Who made him, Adam could have attained to a higher glory, but he fell short (Romans 3:23).

God could not be satisfied with creatures who served Him as robots, automatically. He made man a free moral agent. But the freedom demanded a choice. There must of necessity be a testing of this man and this woman if they were to prove their fidelity to their God.

Edenic Covenant
(Genesis 1:26-3:24)

The Edenic Covenant was made with Adam and Eve before the fall and was conditional upon obedience. Genesis 2:16, 17. (NLT) " . . .The Lord God warned him (Adam), 'You may freely eat the fruit of every tree in the garden – except the tree of the knowledge of good and evil. If you eat its fruit, you are sure to die.'"

God's prohibition against eating of the "tree of the knowledge of good and evil" was not motivated by fear that human knowledge might become equal to His own. It was aimed at frustrating any attempt on the part of the man and woman to pursue their own way in life. God's warning was clear. Sin would bring severe spiritual consequences. Although Adam and Eve did not die on the spot when they violated this command, they did suffer immediate spiritual death that later led to physical death. From their story, believers can know that although our eternal relationship with God is forever secure, sin affects our fellowship with the Father and can lead to far greater consequences unless we repent.

This covenant of God with man, contains seven points, and outlines specifically man's work, the conditions of continued blessing, and the consequences of disobedience.

Articles of the Covenant

Man was to:
1. "Be fruitful, and multiply, and replenish the earth."
2. Subdue the earth for his use: (food and shelter)
3. Take dominion over the lower orders of creation, the animals (1:38)
4. Be vegetarian (1:29) (eat fruit and vegetables)
5. Take care of the garden (2:15) (work for his sustenance)
6. The test: Man was not to eat of the tree of knowledge of good and evil. (to obey God's command)
7. The punishment: Death (2:17). Adam's failure under this covenant resulted in his expulsion from the Garden of Eden and in the Fall of the Human race from a state of innocence into a condition characterized by sin. Their spiritual death began at that moment and eventually led to their physical deaths.

Man breaks the Edenic Covenant

Satan entered the Garden of Eden to tempt man. The serpent was the first creature on this new earth to yield to Satan. Genesis 3:1 tells how the serpent was more subtle than any beast of the field which the Lord God had made. He loaned his body to Satan and became a mouthpiece for him. This, beyond doubt, refers to a literal serpent, as we do not find anywhere in the Bible where the devil has the power to turn himself into a serpent or any other beast.

We must remember that one of God's commands to Adam was to "have dominion over" the animal kingdom. If Eve had remembered and heeded this, she might have refused the voice of Satan which came to her through one of the animals over which man was to have dominion or rule. Instead, as she listened, the serpent, used of Satan, dominated her thoughts and actions, and deceived her.

Satan's tactics then, as now, consisted in asserting authority where he did not actually have the right to do so. He used the serpent over which Eve should have asserted dominion. "Resist the devil, and he will flee from you", would have worked for Eve, and it will work for us today.

Satan continued his attack by casting doubt on God's Word. God had prophesied, "In the day that thou eatest thereof, thou shalt surely die." Satan added only one word: "Ye shall **not** surely die."

He is still at the business of disparaging the Word of God. If the tactic was so successful when used on a perfect creature like Eve, how much more will he seek to use it on us who were sinners saved by grace?

After casting a doubt on God's Word, Satan continued to weaken Eve by casting a reflection on the integrity of God, ascribing ulterior motives to Him: "For God doth know that in the day ye eat thereof, then your eyes shall be opened, and ye shall be as gods, knowing good and evil."

He is still at this business – denying that God's ways are best, and causing men to doubt His goodness, because they do not see His ultimate purposes.

Eve was enticed by these smooth words of the enemy, and by the attractiveness of the fruit on which he focused her attention for too long. She ate, and "gave also unto her husband with her; and he did eat". (Genesis 3:6)

Results of the Fall

The results of the Fall were of two kinds, immediate and long range.

Immediate Results. Satan usually inserts a half-truth or a distortion of truth into his lies to make them more attractive. One of these half-truths that had appealed to Eve was, "Your eyes shall be opened." That much was true. But they saw, not some great knowledge or secret that God in cruelty had concealed from them. What they saw was only that they were naked, and because sin had entered their hearts, they felt instinctively that they should be clothed.

Prior to the Fall, both Adam and Eve had been clothed with the shining glory of God. After the Fall, the glory of God left them, and for the first time, they could see their nakedness. The pristine purity of these persons, created in the image of God, was gone forever now. Their immediate need for clothing precluded their searching out any of the other secrets God had presumably kept from them. So they settled down to the mundane task of making aprons of fig leaves. What a letdown that must have been from the great ideas Satan had put into Eve's mind.

Evening came on and, for the first time they did not welcome the voice of their Creator. Had Eve thought, as she ate the fruit, that she would accuse God when He came that evening, of keeping some very interesting knowledge from them? If she had, the thought had fled some time during the afternoon. Not even the fig leaf aprons seemed sufficient to cover them from God, in whose Presence they had been so comfortable before.

So "Adam and Eve hid themselves from the Presence of the Lord God, amongst the trees of the garden." And when God called, "Adam, where art thou?", God knew where they were hiding, but He wanted them to realize where they were in their relationship with Him. Adam could not keep still, so, bit by bit, the sordid story came out. However, Adam blamed both

Eve and God. He blamed God for "the woman thou gavest me."

Long-range Results. All involved in this disobedience shared in the pronouncement of judgment, which was peculiarly suited to each one. God began with the serpent. Genesis 3:14-19 (NLT) "Then the Lord God said to the serpent, 'Because you have done this, you are cursed more than all animals, domestic and wild. You will crawl on your belly, groveling in the dust as long as you live. And I will cause hostility between you and the woman, and between your offspring and her offspring. He will strike your head, and you will strike his heel.' (Before the Fall, the serpent must have walked upright). This curse will still be upon the serpent in the Millennium (Isaiah 65:25).

Adamic Covenant

It is evident that the next verse, while referring to the serpent, also defers to Satan. The law of double reference appears here. The serpent is the visible one addressed, but Satan, the invisible, is also included.

The serpent, or snake, is naturally repulsive to man, but something more is involved here. This is the first promise of redemption to be found in the Bible.

"I will put enmity between thee and the woman, and between thy seed and her seed; it shall

bruise thy head, and thou shalt bruise his heel"
(Genesis 3:15).

How meticulously accurate is this phrase,
"seed of the woman," when referring to Christ,
for He was conceived of the Holy Spirit and
born of a virgin.

Now the woman hears her judgment, in verse
16: "I will sharpen the pain of your pregnancy,
and in pain you will give birth. And you will
desire to control your husband, but he will rule
over you.'

To Adam, God says, "Since you listened to
your wife and ate from the tree whose fruit I
commanded you not to eat, the ground is
cursed because of you. All your life you will
struggle to scratch a living from it. It will grow
thorns and thistles for you, though you will eat
of its grains".

By the sweat of your brow will you have food to
eat until you return to the ground from which
you were made. For you were made from
dust, and to dust you will return.'"

This agreement was made with Adam and Eve
after the fall and before the expulsion from the
garden. It ushered in the Dispensation of
Conscience. The covenant consisted of two
parts:

1 - The five fold curse on

    A. The serpent (Genesis 3:14-15; Isaiah 65:25).
    B. Satan (Genesis 3:15; John 12:31; Colossians 2:14-17; Hebrews 2:14-18)
    C. The woman (Genesis 3:16; 1 Corinthians 11:3; 14:34; Timothy 2:11-15)
    D. The man (Genesis 3:17-19; Psalm 90:9-10; Romans 5:12-21)
    E. Theground (Genesis 3:17-19; Romans 8:18-23).

2.- The Promise (Genesis 3:15). This included redemption and the removal of the curse (Romans 8:18-23; Revelation 22:3).

Verse 15 – Part of God's curse on Satan was the inauguration of a state of permanent enmity between his followers and God's followers. Unbelievers hate God and , by extension, those who belong to Him and seek to follow His ways. But this word of curse contained a hint of ultimate blessing. God declared that the conflict between Satan's followers and God's come to a head one day when one of Eve's offspring would crush the head of the serpent at the cost of a wound to His heel. Christians throughout the ages have seen this verse as a prophecy of the work of Christ. His suffering and death were wrenching for Him, but death could not hold Him; He rose again on the third day. For Satan, however, the cross brought about complete and total defeat.

The Fall subjected creation to bondage. The first couple's disobedience incurred a divine curse by which God doomed the woman to intense pain and suffering in childbirth and placed a curse on the ground that made man's work difficult. Clearly God disciplines the disobedient. This is because God's standard is nothing short of sinlessness. However, only one person, our Lord Jesus Christ, has achieved that standard; we sin daily in manifold ways. Our goal and inner desire should be to please God through obedience. When we succumb to temptation, if we are truly repentant, God forgives our sin. However, as in the case of Adam and Eve, He may let us live with the consequences of our disobedience as a reminder to obey Him in the future.

The chapter closes with Adam and Eve clothed with coats of skins made by a loving God, Who tempers His judgment with mercy. They are then driven from the Garden, and an angel is placed there to protect the Tree of Life, lest man should eat of it and live forever in his sinful state.

In the day man ate of the forbidden fruit, he died a spiritual death, which brings on physical death. Physical death brings eternal death and separation from God, unless we are born again of the Spirit of God.

At the end of the Millennium, death will be destroyed. Then man can live forever in his natural body, just as Adam and Eve lived, and could have been alive today if they had not sinned. It was through this awful tragedy that the whole world was cursed. The animal kingdom was also changed. This curse will be lifted from the earth and the animals in the Millennium (Isaiah 11:1-9; 35:1-8; Romans 8:19-23).

Whether Adam and Eve were ever reconciled to God or not, is not revealed in the Bible.

CHAPTER III

DISPENSATION OF CONSCIENCE
(Genesis 3:22-8:14)

This dispensation covered the time span from the Fall to the Flood of Noah, which covered approximately 1,656 years. The number of years is arrived at by following the genealogy in Genesis 5:1-29 to the birth of Noah, then adding 600 years, since Genesis 7:6 gives Noah's age as he entered the ark at 600 years

Man lost his God-conscience at the Fall, along with his innocence, and gained a self-conscience. Conscience is an individual matter, for it is a man's knowledge or concept of right or wrong, and is based on what he has been taught or has observed. It is a built-in warning system, providing for self-judgment which approves or reproves everything we do. It may or may not line up with the Word of God. It can be educated or trained to recognize good and evil, but its action is involuntary.

The old saying, "Let your conscience be your guide," is not always reliable. It is only trustworthy when it is made alive by the Holy Spirit, and in harmony with God's plan.

The dispensation of conscience was based on Adam's limited experience with good and evil.

He should have remembered the positive results of obedience and the disastrous consequences of disobedience.

This dispensation demonstrates what mankind will do if left to his own will and conscience, which have been tainted by the inherited sin nature. The five major aspects of this dispensation are (1) a curse on the serpent, (2) a change in womanhood and childbearing, (3) a curse on nature, (4) the imposing of work on mankind to produce food, and (5) the promise of Christ as the seed who will bruise the serpent's head (Satan's).

Man was tested during this time to see if he would obey his own conscience regarding right and wrong (Genesis 6:1-7; Romans 2:12-16). There were no written laws. The Ten Commandment5s had not been given to Adam in the previous dispensation. His only law was not to eat of the tree of the knowledge of good and evil; and after being driven out of the garden, he did not even have that law (Romans 5:12-14). This dispensation could be called the age of freedom, for man was free to do as he pleased until it became necessary for God to interfere.

The conscience, freedom of the will (without restraint and compulsion to choose right or wrong), and the malice of the devil were all the means of God to bring man to a place of utter dependence upon Him for help and redemption from the curse.

The conscience demonstrated how exceedingly sinful man would become if he chose evil instead of good; the full freedom of action demonstrated how far man would go in his rebellion against God before it would be necessary for Him to interfere for the good of His own eternal plan; and the malice of satanic forces demonstrated the contrast between the two masters whom man might serve while on probation. Such freedom of the will and conscience was what man chose in the fall; and so God permitted him to go to the full limit of wickedness that he might learn the folly of his own choice, and that all coming generations might profit thereby.

The Adamic Covenant was introduced in Genesis 3:15. Under the covenant:

1. The serpent was cursed (3:14).
2. God promised redemption through the seed of the woman (3:15);
3. The woman experienced multiplied sorrow and pain in childbearing (3:16);
4. The earth was cursed (3:17,18);
5. Sorrow, pain and physical death became part of the experience of life.
6. Labor became burdensome (3::19).

Man failed under this covenant, degenerating to the point where people did only evil continually until God judged them with the Flood.

Cainic Covenant

Genesis 4:11-15 (NLT) "God said to Cain, "Now you are cursed and banished from the ground, which has swallowed your brother's blood. No longer will the ground yield good crops for you, no matter how hard you work! From now on you will be a homeless wanderer on the earth."

Cain replied to the Lord, 'My punishment is too great for me to bear! You have banished me from the land and from Your presence; you have made me a homeless wanderer. Anyone who finds me will kill me!'

The Lord replied, 'No, for I will give a sevenfold punishment to anyone who kills you.' Then the Lord put a mark on Cain to warn anyone who might try to kill him."

This was a pledge to Cain of vengeance on anyone who found him and killed him.

God banished Cain from his farmland and declared that it would no longer yield crops for him. This punishment hit Cain hard, for he was a man of the land who had offered God produce he had raised himself.   His descendants became a nomadic people with nowhere to settle, a family of fugitives. By his own admission, Cain also lost access to God's presence.   But God promised Cain earlier (Genesis 4:7) that if he responded with the right attitude, he would be accepted.   It was

Cain's choice, then, to be a self-made man with nowhere to call home.

Cain was afraid other people would hurt him. We don't know who these other people were – probably descendants of Adam and Eve's other children. We also don't know the exact nature of Cain's "mark" or how anyone else was to recognize and understand it. But since Cain's punishment was worse than he could imagine, he must have felt some reassurance in knowing that an even more terrible retribution awaited any enemies he encountered. While Cain failed to submit to God's leadership, he accepted God's power to dole out his punishment.

Judgment –the Flood

Whatever Adam and Eve had thought there was to be gained by knowledge of good and evil, they could hardly have imagined that their failure in the Garden would have brought the world so soon to such a wicked state. Only 1,656 years from the time they were driven from the Garden, "God saw that the wickedness of man was great in the earth, and that every imagination of the thoughts of his heart was only evil continually... The earth also was corrupt before God, and ...filled with violence" (Genesis 6:5, 11).

Only Noah found grace in the eyes of the Lord, and God gave him instructions for preparing an ark for the preservation of his family.

In Genesis 6:3 is a statement which is often misinterpreted to mean that it took Noah 120 years to build the ark: (KJV) "And the LORD said, 'My spirit shall not always strive with man, for that he also is flesh: yet his days shall be an hundred and twenty years."

This prophecy was fulfilled in Adam, and God gave him 120 more years to live before being cut off. This was given when Adam was 810 years old, making verses 1-2 refer to the 810 years since Adam's creation, and verse 4 refer to the days after this to the flood.

The word <u>man</u> in verse 3 is translated from the Hebrew word ADAM, with the definite article, the man Adam. The meaning is, "for that he (Adam) is <u>also</u> flesh (as all other men are): yet his (Adam's) days shall be an hundred and twenty years". If <u>man</u> is held to be in the plural, meaning all humans in general, and not Adam in particular, then who else is referred to by the word <u>also</u>? The fact is, the verse reveals that Adam had corrupted his way upon earth, as all other flesh had done, and that God, in His mercy, gave Adam 120 more years in which to repent and conform his life to the will of his Creator. We have no record that he did repent.

So God did not decree that humans would live to be 120 years old. How long you live depends on many factors, such as: genetics, lifestyle, the food you eat, toxics in the geographic place you live, being accident free, not fighting in wars and many other factors, including the strength of your immune system and the diseases you avoid.

A close study of the facts shows that God was not referring to the length of time in which the ark would be built, in Genesis 6:3 either. Noah was at least 500 years old before his sons were born (Genesis 5:32), He was 600 years old when the Flood came and , according to Genesis 6:9-22, these sons were born before God told him to build the ark. Verse 18 shows that they were also grown and had taken wives by that time. We read in Genesis 11:10 that Shem was 98 years old when the Flood ended, so the ark had to be built in much less than 97 years. How much less we do not know, but we do know it could not possibly have been 120 years in the building.

Again, even in the midst of judgment, we see God's hand of mercy. He permitted Noah to preach all the time he was preparing the ark, but men chose to ignore his warning.

In God's instructions to Noah, He made provision for the continuation of animal sacrifice after the Flood. God knew what men may not have perceived – that, while Noah was the only righteous one on the earth, there was within him and his children the seed of Adam's sin. He would need a sacrifice even beyond the Flood.

God provided the means for that sacrifice when He instructed Noah to save more of the clean animals than the unclean (Genesis 6:9 -7:3).

CHAPTER IV

DISPENSATION OF HUMAN GOVERNMENT
(GENESIS 8:15 – 11:9)

From the time of the Flood until Abram's call at the age of 75 years, was 427 years. (See Genesis 11:10-32) For genealogical record of the years then, see Abraham's age at his call (Genesis 12:4).

There are several similarities between the beginning of this dispensation and the beginning of the last dispensation, the dispensation of conscience.

1. A catastrophe has placed a small group of people in a new environment, in which they must make a new life under a new covenant.

2. God gave to each the task of replenishing the earth. In other words, they were to fill it up as it had already been in some previous time.

3. They had each seen firsthand that sin brings punishment.

4. Each knew how to approach God through sacrifice.

But each dispensation brings with it an added revelation of God, and the greater light brings greater responsibility.

Noah was 601 years old when he came out of the Ark. He knew God's plan and began the new dispensation in the right way – by building an altar to God and offering burnt offerings.

"And the Lord smelled a sweet savor, and the Lord said in His heart, I will not again curse the ground any more for man's sake; . . . neither will I again smite any more every thing living as I have done. While the earth remaineth, seed time and harvest, and cold and heat, and summer and winter, and day and night shall not cease" (Genesis 8:21-22).

Noah and his family and all the animals were in the Ark for 1 year and 17 days. Dake, in his Annotated Reference Bible tells about the size of Noah's Ark:. "Considering a cubit (Genesis 6:15) is 25 inches, the Ark was about 625 feet long, 104 feet wide, and 62.5 feet high. Up to AD 1850, there was no ship in the history of the world as large as the Ark. Of the world's steamships up to 1932, less than 1 percent were as large, and only 160 were longer, 7 wider and 8 higher than the Ark. Only 6 had a greater tonnage. The capacity of the Ark was equivalent in tonnage to more than 600 freight cars, which would form a train about 4 miles long, capable of handling over 90,000,000 pounds.

The Ark was easily large enough for all it was to hold. The fish and other sea creatures stayed in the sea; insects were small as well as snakes and lizards. The average size of most mammals was no larger than a dog. The birds could have easily lodged in the ceilings or been hung up in cages. An ox is allowed 20 square feet on a modern vessel. If this much room was allowed in the Ark for each of the larger mammals, there would have been ample room for all, including food for a year and 17 days."

Dake also talks about the "window" of the Ark (Genesis 6:16). "The Hebrew word TSOHAR means an opening or place for light 'with lower, second, and third stories shalt thou make it." This is not CHALLOWN, translated window in Genesis 8:6, which means one of the windows in TSOHAR, the place for light on each of the three decks. TSOHAR is also translated as noontide in Jeremiah 20:16; noonday in Deuteronomy 28:29, Job 5:14; 11:17; Psalm 37:6; Isaiah 16:3; Jeremiah 15:8; and noon in Genesis 43:16,25; 2 Samuel 4:5; 1 Kings 18:26, 27; 20:16. In no Scripture are we told that there was only one small opening in the roof where all the odors of so many animals and the refuse would be removed.

We have no passage indicating that God required men and thousands of animals to live in a tight place without light, ventilation and sanitation for one year and seventeen days. Recent archaeological findings in Nippur disclose that the ark had a sewage system

40

unsurpassed by that of any modern city, and that there were openings for light and ventilation in each story.

Now, at long last, God opens the door as the ark rests on the top of the Ararat Mountains in modern day Turkey, and a new dispensation begins.

New Laws and Conditions

It is as if God says to Noah, "Now this is your chance to start a better order of things. You can do better if you will obey My laws. I will show you how to govern yourselves."

In Genesis 9:3, God gives mankind a new diet. From Adam to Noah most people were vegetarians, but God now says, "Every moving thing that lives shall be meat (food) for you; even as the green herb have I given you all things. God gave man permission for the first time to do what Jabal had already done; to eat meat as well as vegetables.

But in verse 4 there is a restriction. "But flesh with the life thereof, which is the blood thereof, shall you not eat." Man is to eat no blood, a reminder that blood is the vehicle of redemption to come.

When God gave man a vegetable diet, He retained the Tree of Knowledge to attest His own supreme lordship, and to remind Adam of the conditions of his tenure. Now, with animal food permitted, He likewise retained a portion (the blood) to testify that He alone is the giver of all life.

Later, Moses was to link blood with redemption (Numbers 17:11), when he would explain, "For the life of the flesh is in the blood . . . it is the blood that makes an atonement for the soul."

God again gave man dominion over the beasts of the earth, reminding him that he is a higher order of creation.

One of the most significant laws God put into effect under the Dispensation of Human Government was the law of capital punishment as a means of dealing with murderers. "Whoso sheddeth man's blood, by man shall his blood be shed: for in the image of God made He man" (Genesis 9:6).

The law of capital punishment is mentioned as continuing under the Dispensation of Law: "He that smiteth a man, so that he die, shall surely be put to death" (Exodus 21:12).

Paul also acknowledged capital punishment in the Dispensation of Grace, in Romans 13:4. Verse 4 (KJV), "For he is the minister of God to thee for good. But if you do that which is evil, be afraid; for he beareth not the sword in vain: for he is the minister of God, an avenger to execute wrath (capital punishment) upon him that does evil."

The purpose of human government is supposed to uphold the good and punish the evil. Of course, there must be moral leadership for this to be accomplished. Right and wrong, by law, is determined by the state and federal governments. The Christian citizen is to fear and obey the government, as long as the government does not demand citizens to violate God's Word.

Paul states that governmental officials hold office by virtue of God's appointment, and are primarily the servants of God in their offices. However, many politicians think they are the ruling class and the masses are beneath them. Politicians should be the servants of the people. We still must honor the "office" even if we can't honor the people in the "office". The political leader should actively uphold the good.

The "sword" is a symbol representing the authority given to government to protect its citizens by punishing those who do what it has determined is wrong. I think it is important for Christians to be actively involved in government so that the government's values are consistent with the Word of God.

Under the Law of Moses, there were forty-two Death-Penalty sins:

1. murder
2. failing to circumcise
3. eating leavened bread during the feast of unleavened bread
4. smiting parents

5. cursing parents
6. kidnapping
7. negligence with animals that kill
8. witchcraft
9. bestiality
10. idolatry
11. making holy anointing oil
12. putting holy anointing oil on strangers
13. making the holy perfume
14. defiling the Sabbath
15. working on the Sabbath
16. eating the flesh of the peace offering in uncleanness
17. eating the fat of sacrifices
18. killing sacrifices other than at the door of the tabernacle.
19. eating blood
20. incest
21. eating sacrifices at the wrong time
22. consecration of children to idols
23. spiritualism
24. adultery
25. sodomy – homosexuality
26. relationship with a menstruous woman
27. whoredom
28. sacrilege
29. refusing to fast on Day of Atonement
30. working on Day of Atonement
31. blasphemy
32. failure to keep the Passover
33. presumptuous sins
34. gathering firewood on the Sabbath
35. failure to purify self before worship
36. false prophecy

37. leading people away from God
38. backsliding
39. stubbornness and rebellion
40. gluttony
41. drunkenness
42. false dreams and visions

In Romans 13:1-4, God has delegated authority, even under Grace, to defend the good and punish evil – even with capital punishment, if required.

The one who does evil ought to fear. The authority does not carry the "sword" without a purpose. It is clear that God has ordained force to be used by human authorities to prevent anarchy and the tyranny of evil in human society.

The method of human government is in contrast with God's dealing with Cain under the Dispensation of Conscience. With this new God-given authority of man over man for the first time, is implied the whole range of human government. Other laws were added in this and other dispensations, but this is where human government began. There were certain other civil laws that later sprang forth from the Babylonian code which governed the people from Persia to the Caspian Sea and the Mediterranean area. These were not of divine origin. They concerned such matters as adoption; concubines (Genesis 16:1-3; 30:1-24); burial places; taking of life by burning;

death for stealing from a palace; special portions to a favorite son, etc.

The Noahic Covenant

God made the following promises and commands to Noah and his family:
1. God will not curse the earth again.
2. Noah and family are to replenish the earth with people.
3. They shall have dominion over the animal creation.
4. They are allowed to eat meat.
5. The law of capital punishment is established.
6. There never will be another worldwide flood.
7. The sign of God's promise will be the rainbow.

Noah's descendants did not scatter and fill the earth as God had commanded, thus failing in their responsibility in this dispensation.

Genesis 8:20-9:29. This contract was made with Noah and the beasts of the field after the flood, and ushered in the Dispensation of Human Government. The terms of the covenant were:

1. That God would not curse the ground or living creatures any more "while the earth remained." Genesis 8:22; 9:12, 16 (NLT) "As long as the earth remains,

46

there will be planting and harvest, cold and heat, summer and winter, day and night."

"Then God said, 'I am giving you a sign of My covenant with you and with all living creatures, for all generations to come.'" "When I see the rainbow in the clouds, I will remember the eternal covenant between God and every living creature on earth."

Let the seasons remind you that we serve a God who providentially keeps His promises.

What did the rainbow mean? The Flood may have represented the first occurrence of rain on the earth. If so, the rainbow God placed in the sky was likely the first one ever seen by human beings. Perhaps the rainbow was a symbol of beauty made from what had been destructive. More than a natural phenomenon, however, it stood as a sign between God and all living creatures. Since the Hebrew word for rainbow can also be used to refer to a bow – as in a bow used to shoot arrows – some have said that the rainbow was an image of God hanging up His bow in the sky, declaring no more destruction of humanity. Finally, following the archery analogy, it could represent God pointing a war-bow at Himself, forever reminding us that He would sooner perish than break His promises to us.

2. That man should replenish the earth forever. Genesis 9:1 (NLT) "Then God blessed Noah and his sons and told them, 'Be fruitful and multiply. Fill the earth.'"

God gave dominion over the earth and commanded him and his family to multiply and fill the world with people again. These were the same responsibilities God conferred upon Adam. Interestingly, He now granted the living creatures to humanity for food, whereas earlier He had dictated that the diet of Adam and Eve and their children should consist of fruit and vegetable only (Genesis 1:29). The only requirement was that they should not eat animals with the lifeblood in them. Leviticus gives two reasons for this strange requirement. First, refraining from eating blood shows respect for the sanctity of life. Second, it is by blood that atonement for sin must be made.

3. That man should rule the earth. Genesis 9:2-3 (NLT) "All the animals of the earth, all the birds of the sky, all the small animals that scurry along the ground, and all the fish in the sea will look on you with fear and terror. I have placed them in your power. I have given

them to you for food, just as I have given you grain and vegetables."

4. That animals should be eaten, but not the blood. Genesis 9:4 (NLT) "But you must never eat any meat that still has the lifeblood in it."

5. That there should be capital punishment for murderers. Genesis 9:5-6 (NLT) "And I will require the blood of anyone who takes another person's life. If a wild animal kills a person, it must die. And anyone who murders a fellow human must die. If anyone takes a human life, that person's life will also be taken by human hands. For God made human beings in his own image."

The value of human life. God clearly states that murder is forbidden. To break this law deserves capital punishment. Why? Because human beings are created in the very image of God. Thus, to take the life of another human being is to attack the Creator God. Imagine that someone destroyed something you had made and cherished. Would you not feel as though you had been personally attacked? This simple analogy, however, does not capture the seriousness of murder. God values life, and humans are the pinnacle of His creation. There is no clearer way to assault the Creator than to destroy a living person – His finest creation. (Also see Numbers 35)

6. That the rainbow should be a sign of the covenant. (Genesis 9:12-17)
7. That the covenant would be eternal. (Genesis 9:12, 16)

Man greatly needed this reassurance at this time when he was beginning the adventure of human government. God knew by foreknowledge that man would miserably fail in this also, and He began to show His great mercy, which would climax in the sending of His Son in another dispensation. With the evidences of the Flood still around them, man would naturally wonder if it could happen again, and how soon. So God's covenant had a special comfort for that generation.

Failure

In spite of man's new beginning, there was soon evidence of failure. Noah, the preacher of righteousness, became drunk and disgraced himself in the eyes of his own son. Ham, acting in complete disrespect for his father, also failed (Genesis 9:20-27).

There have been many conclusions that surround verse 24. It says (KJV), "And Noah awoke from his wine, and knew what his younger son had done unto him." Many believe that Ham, or possibly his grandson, Canaan, had a homosexual experience with

Noah as he lay in a drunken stupor, naked in his tent. If someone had only looked at him, how would Noah have known what was actually done to him? Would just a look have prompted Noah to curse Ham, his son, Canaan, and many who would be born into Ham's lineage?

The Canaanites were white. In no way is this to be interpreted as a curse on the black race. The Canaanites practiced ritual prostitution, homosexuality, and various orgiastic rites, and were the center of God's prophecy of judgment in Genesis 15:16, to be carried out by Israel after their sojourn in Egypt. But the curse did not preclude individual salvation, for Rahab joined Israel, and Hiram, king of Tyre, gave materials for the building of Solomon's Temple.

When Noah realized what had happened, he pronounced a curse upon Ham, and, prophetically, a blessing upon Shem. Through Shem, the Savior was to come, and it is a line that is traced throughout Genesis. This may account for the fact that he is listed last in the genealogies of Noah's sons, given in chapter 10 of Genesis. (He was actually the middle son.)

All the European races are through Japheth's lineage. Everyone on the planet today can be traced back to Noah, through his three sons.

The Tower of Babel

Perhaps out of disbelief of God's promise that He would not again destroy the earth by water, man had a lurking fear that the terror of the Flood might be repeated. At least, from some apparently self-preserving instinct, coupled with rebellion, they decided to build a tower, a central meeting place, a symbol of their unity, "lest we be scattered abroad upon the face of the whole earth" (Genesis 11:4).

This was the beginning of centralized government. The Hebrew expression translated, "Let us make us a name" (verse 4), has in it the thought of open rebellion. As is necessary for all rebellions, there was an agitator, a leader. Nimrod evidently had a powerful and evil personality. He was able to rally men about him and to dazzle them with his feats of strength.

Nimrod's name means "Let Us Revolt." Arab traditions record ruins named after him at Birs-Nimrod, which is Borsippa, and at the Nimrud of Calan. His activities centered first in Shinar (Babylonia) and included building the Tower of Babel (Genesis 11:1-9). Then he went to Assyria (see Micah 5:6).

Some believe that since the context deals with men and not animals, his prowess in hunting deals with men and that his exploits are of a moral and spiritual nature. "Mighty Hunter" is from Genesis 6:4, and his name relates to the word MARAD, meaning "rebel". Thus he established a thoroughly autocratic imperialistic, despotic system of government (of a kind described in Isaiah 13 and 14), back of which stands Satan in all his rage against God. He did all of this before the Lord. What he did was very significant and was a matter of concern to God Himself. God certainly knows what everybody does; but this made a strong impression on God.

While Nimrod instigated the building of the Tower of Babel, his evil wife, Simeramis, led the people into a mystical religion centered upon her own personality and that of her son, whom she claimed was supernaturally conceived by her having intercourse with a god.

The Tower of Babel was built in the land of Shinar in Mesopotamia, which seems to have been the location also of some of the earth's earliest cities.

According to ancient Babylonian descriptions, the tower contained shrines to many gods, so it is the earliest evidence of idolatry. The same tablet which gives this information also says that this building apparently offended "the gods", for they 'came down and in a night threw down what they had built."

The Bible does not record that the tower was destroyed. Dake records: "A Babylonian description of the tower of Babel, discovered in 1876, indicates there was a grand court 900 feet x 1,156 feet, and a smaller one, 450 feet x

1,056 feet, inside of which was a platform with walls about it, having four gates on each side. In the center stood the tower with many small shrines at the base, dedicated to various gods. The tower itself was 300 feet high with decreased width in stages, from the lowest to the highest point. Each was square. The first foundation stage measured 300 feet square and 110 feet high; the second measured 260 feet square and 60 feet high; the third, 200 feet square and 20 feet high; the fourth, 170 feet square and 20 feet high; the fifth, 140 feet square and 20 feet high; the sixth, 110 feet square and 20 feet high; and the seventh, 80 feet long, 60 feet wide, and 50 feet high. On the top platform, measuring 60 feet x 80 feet, was a sanctuary for the god, Bel-Merodach, and signs of the zodiac. The builders evidently finished the tower, for the work was stopped on the city only."

After the Flood, God wanted people to spread out and repopulate the earth, but the people wanted to stay in one location, and they rebelled against God and began creating their own "gods" and became very evil.

In Genesis 11:7-9, God enforced His will over their wills, and two things happened: He confounded their languages. By that act, it caused people to gather in groups that could communicate with each other. These various groups began to scatter around the planet to start their own nations.

What men will not do willingly, God forces them to do as a result of judgment. Today there are more than three thousand languages and dialects.

In Genesis 10:25, it states that, in Peleg's day, the earth was divided. For many, many years, the earth was not divided by vast oceans like it is now. God was making it impossible for the scattered groups of people to reunite into one location ever again. This could explain how the ancient Indian civilizations of the North and South American continents flourished even before other nations were aware of the existence of either the people or the great continents.

On a map of the world, you can notice that the west coast of Africa and Europe could fit roughly into the eastern coastline of our hemisphere. This would indicate the separation or dividing of what had once been a very vast land area, by water.

The Dispensation of Human Government began with bright promise as Noah sacrificed to Jehovah, "and the Lord smelled a sweet savor."

Now, 427 years later, the dispensation closes in idolatry and rebellion.

CHAPTER V

THE DISPENSATION OF PROMISE
(Genesis 11:10 – Exodus 12:41)

This fourth dispensation started with the call of Abraham, continued through the lives of the patriarchs, and ended with the Exodus of the Jewish people from Egypt, a period of about 430 years. During this dispensation, God developed a great nation that He had chosen as His people.

The time period of 430 years is mentioned three times in Scripture --- Exodus 12:40-41; Galatians 3:17. The time is reckoned from Abram's call at age 75 to the time of the deliverance of the children of Israel from Egyptian bondage. Broken down, this allows 25 years from Abraham's call to the birth of Isaac (Genesis 21:5); 60 years to the birth of Jacob (Genesis 25:26); 147 years of Jacob's life (Genesis 47:28); 54 years between Jacob's and Joseph's deaths (Genesis 37:2; 41:46; 47:28; 50:22).. From Joseph's death to the deliverance from Egypt was 144 years (Exodus 1:40; Galatians 3:14-17).

In Genesis 11:10-32, there is a detailed genealogy of Abram, leading back to Noah's son, Shem. As Noah was the tenth generation from Adam, so Abram was the tenth from Noah.

The name (Dispensation of Promise) was because of the promises and covenants made with Abraham and his seed. In this period, God began to predict and emphasize the coming of the seed of the woman to be through a particular branch of the race. There had been a few predictions before, but now Abraham's seed was designated as the special line through which Christ should come. In this age, many promises and predictions were made to this end.

God now began to deal with a special branch of the race (Abraham's seed) in the fulfillment of His plan. Not only did He promise that the Messiah would come through them, but that the promised land would be given to them eternally, as a base for world missionary and governmental operations, and that the revelation of God should come through them..

The promise of God was to choose one man through whom Messiah should come, to use him and his seed as His representatives in the earth, and to give them Canaan as a base of operation concerning his program among men in the gospel and in government eternally.

The second eruption of the sons of God among men had already begun, and giants were being born. They were beginning to possess the very land God had in mind for His own headquarters on earth. It was His plan to use the sword of Israel to destroy these giants so as to preserve a pure line for Messiah to come through.

God allowed Abraham's offspring to become a great and mighty nation down in Egypt. It was His further purpose to show the heathen, through Abraham, the difference between serving Him and other gods. Also He wanted to make Israel an example to all men physically, mentally, morally, spiritually, and financially, as a nation enjoying the blessings of the true God, so that others should be won to Him by such benefits. Never was the purpose of God expressed more fully and clearly to any people, and never before did a nation have in their power such means of blessing all nations and bringing about universal peace, prosperity, and eternal salvation, as Israel.

The Dispensation of Promise opened with God's call to Abram, as recorded in Genesis 12:1. "Now the LORD had said unto Abram, 'Get thee out of thy country, and from thy kindred, and from thy father's house, unto a land that I will show you;'"

From Acts 7:2, we learn that God first called Abram before he went to Haran. From Joshua 24:2, we learn that Terah and his family were idolaters previous to this call. It was Terah that took Abram and others to go into Canaan. Terah seems to have become converted to Abram's God, and desired to flee idolatry and persecution from his neighbors. God repeats

His call to Abram, which was first given in Ur of the Chaldees (Acts 7:2).

There are several interesting contrasts between this dispensation and those prior to it;
1. Previously, God had dealt with all mankind as a group. There was no singling out of one over another at the beginning of the dispensations.
2. Although there were some inklings of a special line through which the Savior promised in Genesis 3:5 should come, the plan was obscure before the choosing of Abram.
3. No one area had been chosen before as the land which God would use as a base of operations in working out the plan of redemption.
4. The call to separation of the godly from the ungodly was never as plain as it was to Abram.

On the other hand, there were similarities. The testing through which Abram was proved, in the long wait for Isaac, is reminiscent of Noah's building an ark when no one could see the necessity. Both, no doubt, had to endure ridicule, and yet, both were faithful in their time.

Abram seemed content to live in Haran until his father died. When Terah died in Haran, Abram moved on in obedience to his call. He took with him Lot, his dead brother's son, but eventually Lot separated from Abram, pitching his tent toward Sodom. And the very land Lot chose was promised to Abram almost before

Lot could move his herds into its grass and find the waterholes where they could drink.

All his life, Abram was to follow God's call, and embrace a promise he did not live to see completely fulfilled.

God gave these 48 promises to Abraham (all references are in Genesis):
1. I will show you the land (12:1)
2. make you a great nation (12:2)
3. bless you (12:2; 22:17)
4. make your name great (12:2)
5. you will be a blessing (12:2)
6. I will bless them that bless you (12:3)
7. curse them that curse you (12:3)
8. in you all nations will be blessed (12:3; 22:18)
9. I will give this land to your seed forever (12:7; 13:14-17; 15:18-21; 17:8). No matter what the United Nations says, Israel will belong to the seed of Abraham forever.
10. I will make your seed as the dust in number (13:16)
11. I am your shield (15:1)
12. I am your great reward (15:1)
13. your own son shall be your heir (15:2-4)
14. your seed shall be as the stars in number (15:5; 22:17) On a clear night the eye can see about 3,000 stars or suns. There are about 30 billion that astronomers can photograph singly. The multitudes of other stars are so

close together they appear as a solid mass to us.

15. your seed shall be strangers and oppressed 400 years (15:13)
16. I will punish their oppressors (15:14)
17. I will bring your seed out of bondage (15:14-16, fulfilled in Exodus 12).
18. I will bless your seed with great material substance (15:14)
19. you will die in peace (15:15)
20. you will be buried in a good old age (15:15)
21. I will make an eternal covenant with you (17:4, 7)
22. I will multiply you exceedingly (17:2; 22:17)
23. you will be the father of many nations (17:5-6)
24. I will make you exceedingly fruitful (17:6)
25. kings will come from you (17:6)
26. I will make a covenant with your seed eternally (17:7)
27. I will be a God to you and your seed (17:7-8)
28. I will bless your wife (17:16)
29. I will give you a son of her (17:16-19)
30. she shall be a mother of many nations (17:16)
31. king's shall come of her (17:16)
32. I will establish My everlasting covenant with Isaac and his seed (17:19-21)
33. I will bless Ishmael (17:20)
34. I will make him fruitful (17:20)
35. I will multiply him abundantly (17:20)
36. 12 princes shall he beget (17:20)

37. I will make him a great nation (17:20)
38. Sarah shall gave a son next year (17:21: 18:10, 14)
39. I will not destroy Sodom if I find 50 righteous (18:26)
40. I will not destroy the city if I find 45 righteous (18:28)
41. I will not destroy it if I find 40 righteous (18:29)
42. I will not destroy it if I find 30 righteous (18:30)
43. I will not destroy it if I find 20 righteous (18:31)
44. I will not destroy it if I find 10 righteous (18:32)
45. in Isaac shall your seed be called (21:12)
46. I will multiply your seed as the sand in number (22:17)
47. your seed shall be the victor over their enemies (22:17)
48. in your seed shall all nations be blessed (22:18)

The Dispensation of Promise is considered to have started with Abram's going into Canaan after his father's death, and to have ended with the exodus of the children of Israel from Egypt.

What kind of promise did God make that would entice a well-established man to leave his country, his kindred, and his father's house for parts unknown, "a land that I will show thee."? How can a 75 year old childless man expect to become the father of a "great nation"? We cannot know in what manner the Lord appealed to Abram, but we know that it was real enough that he obeyed.

Abram's part of the covenant involved simple faith and obedience. Whatever God promised, Abram was to believe; and whatever God asked, he was to do. So Abram followed when he did not know where God was leading. He built an altar wherever he pitched his tent, so that all would know that this aging, childless man whose invisible God had made fantastic promises to him, still trusted that God. He possibly counted stars on nights when he could not sleep, and remembered that his God said his seed should be as stars for multitudes. Maybe he brushed the sand from his sandals, and every grain reminded him that God had promised him that there would come a time when his descendants should be as the sands of the sea, innumerable.

The promise had a twofold aspect with regard to time. Certain blessings were promised for Abram's lifetime, and others would not be fulfilled until later.

Let us examine the promise that God made to Abram in establishing His covenant with him. The promise was repeated seven times, including the time before Abram left Ur.

The Abrahamic Covenant
Genesis 12:1-7

(NLT) "The Lord had said to Abram, 'Leave your native country, your relatives, and your father's family, and go to the land that I will show you. I will make you into a great nation. I will bless you (receive personal blessings), and make you famous (receive honor), and you will be a blessing to others. I will bless those who bless you and curse those who treat you with contempt. All the families on earth will be blessed through you.' (See Galatians 3:14) We can receive Abraham's blessings!

So Abram departed as the Lord had instructed, and Lot went with him. Abram was seventy-five years old when he left Haran. He took his wife, Sarai, his nephew, Lot, and all his wealth – his livestock and all the people he had taken into his household at Haran – and headed for the land of Canaan. When they arrived in Canaan, Abram traveled through the land as far as Shechem. There he set up camp beside the oak of Moreh. At this time, the area was inhabited by Canaanites.

"Then the Lord appeared to Abram and said, 'I will give this land to your descendants'. And Abram built an altar there and dedicated it to the Lord, Who had appeared to him."

God made a covenant with Abram. A covenant is part promise, part contract. God promised blessings to Abram and asked something of him. What did God promise? He promised to give Abram many descendants and much influence. What did God ask? He asked that Abram go to a certain land and live a certain way. This covenant between Abram and God is the foundation for much of the rest of the Bible. It was upon this agreement that the nation of Israel was established and the Messiah, Jesus, was foretold. It was by Jesus, a descendant of Abraham, that Abraham would be a blessing to "all the families on earth." Through Abram, God displayed the relationship that He desires to have with His creation through faith.

". . . the area was inhabited by Canaanites." The first Canaanites were descendants of Noah's grandson, Canaan, son of Ham. Canaan's descendants comprised eleven groups that lived in Syria and Palestine. In time, however, the term CANAANITES came to be attached to all the people inhabiting the land between Egypt and Asia Minor. God promised part of this land to Abram. Later, when the Israelites began to inhabit this land, God commanded them to completely destroy the Canaanites and their false religious practices and idols. Because they failed to do so, the Israelites were continually led away from God by the Canaanites, consistently neglecting the purity of worship that God asked of them.

According to the Davis Dictionary of the Bible, "The Canaanites were idolaters, they indulged in shameful and abominable vice, they went beyond other nations in practicing human sacrifice."

The Abrahamic covenant was made with Abraham after the confusion of tongues, when God saw that it was impossible to deal with the race as a whole. It ushered in the Dispensation of Promise. The covenant consisted of two parts:

1. The seven-fold promise
   A. "I will make of you a great nation" Genesis 12:1-3; also Genesis 13:16 (NLT) "And I will give you so many descendants that, like the dust of the earth, they cannot be counted!"

   Genesis 17:18-21 (NLT)"So Abraham said to God, 'May Ishmael live under your special blessing!' But God replied, 'No – Sarah, your wife, will give birth to a son for you You will name him Isaac, and I will confirm My covenant with him and his descendants as an everlasting covenant. As for Ishmael, I will bless him also, just as you have asked. I will make him extremely fruitful and multiply his descendants. He will become the father of twelve princes and I will make him a great nation. But My covenant will be confirmed with Isaac, who will be born to you and Sarah about this time next year.'"
   Genesis 24:34-35(NLT) "I am Abraham's servant,' he explained. 'And the Lord has greatly blessed my master; he has become a wealthy man. The Lord has given him flocks of sheep and goats,

herds of cattle, a fortune in silver and gold, and many male and female servants and camels and donkeys.'"

Galatians 3:6-9 (NLT) "In the same way, Abraham believed God, and God counted him as righteous because of his faith. The real children of Abraham, then, are those who put their faith in God.

What's more, the Scriptures looked forward to this time when God would declare the Gentiles to be righteous because of their faith. God proclaimed this good news to Abraham long ago when he said, 'All nations will be blessed through you.' So all who put their faith in Christ share the same blessing Abraham received because of his faith."

B. "Make your name great."
Exodus 2:24-25 (NLT) "God heard their groaning, and He remembered His covenant promise to Abraham, Isaac, and Jacob. He looked down on the people of Israel and knew it was time to act."

God's covenants with people groups always included three main elements: divine benevolence, requirements of human obedience, and consequences God's covenant with Abraham formed the core of the Hebrew identity. In

this covenant,God had promised to reward Abraham's obedience with land, descendents,and honor.
(Genesis 5:17).

God confirmed Abraham's covenant with Abraham's son, Isaac, and with Isaac's son, Jacob (whom God later renamed Israel). Through Jacob, the covenant extended to the 12 patriarchs of Israel, and to their descendants. In accordance with His covenant benevolence, God responded to Israel's cries for help.

Exodus 6:3-8 (NLT) "'I appeared to Abraham, to Isaac, and to Jacob as El-Shaddai – God Almighty – but I did not reveal My name, Yahweh, to them. And I reaffirmed My covenant with them. Under its terms, I promised to give them the land of Canaan,where they were living as foreigners. You can be sure that I have heard the groans of the people of Israel, who are now slaves to the Egyptians. And I am well aware of my covenant with them.

Therefore, say to the people of Israel I am the Lord, I will free you from your oppression and will rescue you from your slavery in Egypt. I will redeem you with a powerful arm and great acts of judgment. I will claim you as My own people, and I will be your God. Then you will know that I am the Lord your God who has freed you from your oppression in Egypt. I will bring you into the land I swore to give to Abraham, Isaac, and Jacob. I will give it to you as your very own possession. I am the Lord!'"

The Lord was faithful to redeem Israel from slavery because of the covenant. He had made with Abraham, and confirmed with Isaac and Jacob.

C "You shall be a blessing". Galatians 3:13-14 (NLT) "But Christ has rescued us from the curse pronounced by the law. When He was hung on the cross, He took upon Himself the curse for our wrongdoing. For it is written in the Scriptures (Deuteronomy 21:23 – Greek Version), 'Cursed is everyone who is hung on a tree'. Through Christ Jesus, God has blessed the Gentiles with the same blessing He promised to Abraham, so that we who are believers might receive the promised Holy Spirit through faith."

Paul explains to the Galatians that there is no escaping condemnation for violating the law – except through Jesus Christ. Paul does not mean that Jesus Christ became wicked, but rather that Jesus legally took on their guilt (Hebrews 4:15). Instead of becoming a curse, the Galatian believers could be considered perfect by trusting in Jesus

Christ's death on the cross in their place.

D. "I will bless them that bless you." Genesis 12:1-3; Matthew 25:31-46 (NLT) (Jesus speaking) "But when the Son of Man comes in His glory, and all the angels with Him, then He will sit upon His glorious throne. All the nations will be gathered in His presence, and He will separate the people as a shepherd separates the sheep from the goats. He will place the sheep at His right hand and the goats at His left.

"Then the King will say to those on His right, 'Come, you who are blessed by My Father, inherit the Kingdom prepared for you from the creation of the world. For I was hungry, and you fed Me. I was thirsty, and you gave Me a drink. I was a stranger, and you invited Me into your home. I was naked, and you gave Me clothing. I was sick, and you cared for Me. I was in prison, and you visited Me.

"Then these righteous ones will reply, 'Lord, when did we ever see You hungry and feed You? Or thirsty and give You something to drink? Or a stranger and show You hospitality? Or naked and give You clothing? When did we ever see You sick or in prison and visit You?

"And the King will say, 'I tell you the truth, when you did it to one of the least of these My brother and sisters, you were doing it to Me!'

"Then the King will turn to those on the left and say, 'Away with you, you cursed ones, into the eternal fire prepared for the devil and his demons. For I was hungry, and you didn't feed Me. I was thirsty, and you didn't give Me a drink. I was a stranger, and you didn't invite Me into your home. I was naked, and you didn't give Me clothing. I was sick and in prison, and you didn't visit Me.'

"Then they will reply, 'Lord, when did we ever see you hungry or thirsty or a stranger or naked or sick or in prison, and not help you?'

"And He will answer, 'I tell you the truth, when you refused to help the least of these My brothers and sisters, you were refusing to help Me.'

"And they will go away into eternal punishment, but the righteous will go into eternal life."

Jesus' commission to His followers is quite clear: we are to "make disciples" of all people (Matthew 28:19-20). We are to address their spiritual needs. But as primary as that call is, we cannot overlook what else is on Jesus' heart – that we show love for our brothers and sisters in Christ by meeting their physical needs, just as if it were Jesus we were helping. We cannot minister simply to people's spiritual needs; our call is to minister to our brothers and sisters in Christ, regarding all their needs. Look around you, what do people need that you are strategically placed to provide? Look into their eyes and see Jesus – then ask yourself how much you can do to help.

E. "I will bless you." Genesis 13:14-18 (NLT) "After Lot had gone, the Lord said to Abraham, 'Look as far as you can see in every direction – north and south, east and west. I am giving all this land, as far as you can see, to you and your descendants as a permanent possession. And I will give you so many descendants that, like the dust of the earth, they cannot be counted! Go and walk through the land in every direction, for I am giving it to you.'

"So Abram moved his camp to Hebron, near the oak grove belonging to Mamre. There he built another altar to the Lord."

It was for this promise that Abram first left his homeland and all his relatives. The land became the greatest possession and hope of Abram's descendants. Abram settled in it, as did his son, Isaac; and Isaac's son, Israel. However, Israel left the land because of famine, and about 400 years passed before God brought the nation of Israel back to reclaim it. God's promise to Abram laid the foundation for many hopes and many conflicts over the land of Israel. Even to this day, God's ancient people – the Jews, are trying to keep the land that God gave them to be a permanent possession.

When God first promised descendants to Abram, it may have seemed like an impossible dream, because Abram and his wife were both beyond normal childbearing years. Their childlessness was probably a source of shame for Abram, for an inheritance – a child to carry on his legacy – was of the utmost importance to every man of the ancient Near East. But even though it seemed impossible, Abram believed God, and God fulfilled His promise. When the family of Abram's grandson Israel (Jacob) entered Egypt during the famine, they numbered only 70. When they returned from Egypt to reclaim their land, they numbered more than 2 million. God's promise to Abram had been fulfilled.

Genesis 15:18-21 (NLT) "So the Lord made a covenant with Abram that day and said, 'I have given this land to your descendants, all the way from the border of Egypt to the great Euphrates River – the land now occupied by the Kenites, Kenizzites, Kadmonites, Hittites, Perizzites, Rephaites, Amorites, Canaanites, Girgashites, and Jebusites.'"

This land was never fully occupied, even in the prosperous reigns of David and Solomon. It will be fully occupied by Israel in the Millennium. (See Ezekiel 47:13-48:29).

Millennial Division of the Land

The land allotments for the 12 tribes of Israel given here, correspond in principle to the division of the land after the conquest under Joshua (Joshua 13-21). But in Ezekiel's description, the land would be portioned quite differently – in horizontal stripes. Each tribe would be positioned either above or below the others, with its territory extending from the eastern to the western borders of the Promised Land. There would be some movement from north to south as well. Zebulon, Issachar, and Gad would be south of Jerusalem.

The city of earthly Jerusalem during the Millennium will be four-square with a wall and 3 gates on each side, and the names of the 12 tribes of Israel on the gates, as in the new heavenly Jerusalem. The great difference will be in the size of the two cities. The earthly one will be about 10-75 miles square, while the new heavenly Jerusalem will be 1500 miles square and the same measurement high.

F. "I will curse them that curse you." (Zechariah 14; Matthew 25:31-46)
In Zechariah 14, we see the last series of images. "The Day of the Lord", is described as a time of ultimate blessing for God's people and ultimate judgment on God's enemies. Such images are common whenever the prophets describe "that day". These blessings and curses were fulfilled at various times in history, but ultimately they will be fulfilled when Jesus returns. The New Testament writers (especially John in Revelation) describe Jesus'second coming with imagery drawn from Zechariah and the other prophets.

Zechariah described, in 14:4-5, God's coming by saying His "feet" will touch the Mount of Olives in Jerusalem. God's coming will split the earth, making a way of escape for His persecuted flock. Earth-shaking images were often used to communicate the awesome power of God when He comes in judgment (see Psalm 18:7-12 and Isaiah 29:5-7). This scene is similar to the imagery of Revelation 16:17-21, which describes God judging His enemies through an earthquake that splits Jerusalem.

G. "In you shall all the nations of the world be blessed."

Deuteronomy 28:8-14 (NLT) "The Lord will guarantee a blessing on everything you do and will fill your storehouses with grain. The Lord your God will bless you in the land He is giving you.

"If you obey the commands of the Lord your God and walk in His ways, the Lord will establish you as His holy people as He swore He would do. Then all the nations of the world will see that you are a people claimed by the Lord, and they will stand in awe of you.

"The Lord will give you prosperity in the land He swore to your ancestors to give you, blessing you with many children, numerous livestock, and abundant crops. The Lord will send rain at the proper time from His rich treasury in the heavens and will bless all the work you do. You will lend to many nations, but you will never need to borrow from them. If you listen to these commands of the Lord your God that I am giving you today, and if you carefully obey them, the Lord will make you the head and not the tail, and you will always be on top and never at the bottom. You must not turn away from any of the commands I am giving you today, nor follow after other gods and worship them."

Isaiah 60:3-5 (NLT) "All nations will come to your light; mighty kings will come to see your radiance. Look and see, for everyone is coming home! Your sons are coming from distant lands; your little daughters will be carried home. Your eyes will shine, and your heart will thrill with joy, for merchants from around the world will come to you. They will bring you the wealth of many lands."

Isaiah 66:18-21 (NLT) "I can see what they are doing, and I know what they are thinking. So I will gather all nations and peoples together, and they will see My glory. I will perform a sign among them. And I will send those who survive to be messengers to the nations – to Tarshish, to the Libyans and Lydians (who are famous as archers), to Tubal and Greece, and to all the lands beyond the sea that have not heard of My fame or seen My glory. There they will declare My glory to the nations. They will bring the remnant of your people back from every nation. They will bring them to My holy mountain in Jerusalem as an offering to the Lord. They will ride on horses, in chariots and wagons, and on mules and camels,' says the Lord. 'And I will appoint some of them to be My priests and Levites. I, the Lord, have spoken!'"

The sign mentioned here was God's imminent act of judgment upon the ungodly. Those who survived God's judgment would be the seed of a new community that would spread the truth of God throughout the nations. The Gentiles would in turn, bring God's people back to their land.

John 8:56-59 (NLT) (Jesus speaking) "'Your father Abraham rejoiced as he looked forward to My coming. He saw it and was glad. "The people said, 'You aren't even fifty years old. How can You say You have seen Abraham?' Jesus answered, 'I will tell you the truth, before Abraham was even born, I Am!' At that point, they picked up stones to throw at Him. But Jesus was hidden from them, and left the Temple."

Jesus did not merely claim that He existed before Abraham, He claimed that He is the Lord, who has eternally existed. Jesus repeatedly claimed to be the God of the Jewish leader, and they tried to kill Him for this, because they believed He was lying and thereby blaspheming the name of the Lord. However, it was not Jesus' time to die, so He hid Himself and departed.

1   Galatians 3:16 (NLT) "God gave the promises to Abraham and his child. And notice that the Scripture doesn't say 'to his children,' as if it meant many

78

descendants. Rather, it says 'to His child" – and that, of course, means Christ."

2.. The sign of the covenant: circumcision (Genesis 17:1-21; Isaiah 24:5)
Genesis 17:10-14 (NLT) "This is the covenant that you and your descendants must keep: each male among you must be circumcised. You must cut off the flesh of your foreskin as a sign of the covenant between Me and you. From generation to generation, every male child must be circumcised on the eighth day after his birth. This applies not only to members of your family, but also to the servants born in your household and the foreign-born servants whom you have purchased. All must be circumcised. Your bodies will bear the mark of My everlasting covenant. Any male who fails to be circumcised will be cut off from the covenant family for breaking the covenant."

Circumcision was practiced by other ancient cultures besides the Hebrews. What set Hebrew circumcision apart was the fact that it was done to infants as the mark of inclusion in God's everlasting covenant. While other cultures practiced circumcision as a rite of passage at puberty, the Israelites used it to identify themselves as God's chosen people. Upon demand, they had to show their penis as their identification card.

Isaiah 24:5 (NLT) "The earth suffers for the sins of its people, for they have twisted God's instructions, violated His laws, and broken his everlasting covenant."

God gave 14 commands to Abram:
1. Get out of your country (Gen. 12:1; Acts 7:2).
2. Leave your relatives (Gen. 12:1).
3. Leave your father's house (Gen 12:1).
4. Go to a land I will show you (Gen. 12:1)
5. Arise, walk through the land (Gen 13:17).
6. Make a sacrifice to Me (Gen.15:9-12).
7. Walk before Me and be perfect (Gen.17:1)
8. Keep My covenant (Gen.17:9-14).
9. Circumcise all your males (Gen. 17:10-14)
10. Circumcise on the 8th day (Gen. 17:12).
11. Call your son's name Isaac (Gen. 17:19)
12. Obey your wife in this matter (Gen. 21:12).
13. Offer Isaac as a sacrifice (Gen. 22:2)
14. Lay not your hand upon Isaac (Gen. 22:12).

The Hagaric Covenant

Genesis 16:7-15 (NLT) "The angel of the Lord found Hagar beside a spring of water in the wilderness, along the road to Shur. The angel said to her, 'Hagar, Sarai's servant, where have you come from, and where are you going?'

"'I', m running away from my mistress, Sarai', she replied. The angel of the Lord said to her, 'Return to your mistress, and submit to her authority.' Then he added, 'I will give you more descendants than you can count.'

"And the angel also said, 'You are now pregnant and will give birth to a son. You are to name him Ishmael (which means "God hears"), for the Lord has heard your cry of distress. This son of yours will be a wild man, as untamed as a wild donkey! He will raise his fist against everyone, and everyone will be against him. Yes, he will live in open hostility against all his relatives."

"Thereafter, Hagar used another name to refer to the Lord, who had spoken to her. She said, 'You are the God who sees me (Hebrew – El Roi).' She also said, 'Have I truly seen the One who sees me?' So that well was named Beer-laha-roi (which means 'well of the Living One who sees me'). It can still be found between Kedesh and Bered.

"So Hagar gave Abram a son, and Abram named him Ishmael. Abram was eighty-six years old when Ishmael was born."

The angels promise to Hagar was very similar to the promise God had made to Abram- many descendants. Descendants were often considered the true wealth of a person. The angel's promise came true in the life of Ishmael – he had 12 sons, just as Isaac did. Although Ishmael lived a nomadic life, he remained connected with Abram's family and took part in Abram's burial. Arab nations of today claim roots in Ishmael. While Ishmael was not the child God had promised to Abram, God did not forsake him.

Hagar's story is a description of God's compassion. Both the name that the angel gave to the child – Ishmael, or "God hears" – and the name that Hagar gave to the spring – "well of the Living One who sees me" – are suggestive of a redeeming experience with God in a time of need. Hagar's encounter with God reminds us that He honors His promises even when His people make messes of their lives. Her story shows that although God was focused on His relationship with Abram and his descendants, His compassion was big enough to encompass others as well.

This was a covenant made with Hagar concerning her seed through Ishmael, Abraham's son. It concerned many generations and was in three parts:

1. Commands:
    A. Return, submit to Sarah
    (Genesis   16:9).

B. Call her son Ishmael, meaning God shall hear (Genesis 16:11).

2. <u>Promises:</u>
A. Seed to be multiplied beyond number (Genesis 16:10; 17:20-22)
B. Ishmael to be blessed and become a great nation (Genesis 17:20; 21:17-18).
C. Ishmael to beget 12 princes (Genesis 17:20; 25:12-18).

3. <u>Prophetical Revelation:</u>
A. Ishmael to be a wild man (Genesis 16:12).
B. His hand to be against every man (Genesis 16:12).
C. Every man's hand to be against him (Genesis 16:12)
D. Ishmael to dwell in the presence of his brethren (Genesis 16:12).

<u>The Sarahic Covenant</u>

Genesis 17:15-19 (NLT) "Then God said to Abraham, 'Regarding Sarai, your wife – her name will no longer be Sarai. From now on her name will be Sarah. And I will bless her and give you a son from her! Yes, I will bless her richly, and she will become the mother of many nations. Kings of nations will be among her descendants.'

"Then Abraham bowed down to the ground, but he laughed to himself in disbelief. 'How could I become a father at the age of 100?' he thought. 'And how can Sarah have a baby when she is ninety years old?' So Abraham said to God, 'May Ishmael live under your special blessing!'

But God replied, 'No – Sarah, your wife, will give birth to a son for you. You will name him Isaac, and I will confirm My covenant with him and his descendants as an everlasting covenant.'"

Both Sarai and Sarah mean "Princess". However, Sarai also means "princely". Whereas Sarah means "Queen of princes" or "Mother of princes" and is the feminine of Sar, a prince.

Abraham laughed. It seems strange that Abraham laughs at the idea of a hundred year old man begetting a son, when his own father was 130 at the time of his birth. Sarah would die when he was 137, but he was able to beget sons long after that (Genesis 25:1-6) Paul states that when Abraham was 100, "He considered not his own body now dead" (Romans 4:19). This laughter is one of doubt, as verse 18 reveals. His plea, "O that Ishmael might live before you!" indicates his wish to adopt him as his heir. The name Isaac means laughter.

Genesis 18:9-15 (NLT) "'Where is Sarah, your wife?' the visitors asked. 'She's inside the tent,' Abraham replied. Then one of them said, 'I will return to you about this time next year, and your wife, Sarah, will have a son!.

"Sarah was listening to this conversation from the tent,. Abraham and Sarah were both very old by this time, and Sarah was long past the age of having children. So she laughed to herself and said, 'How could a worn-out woman like me enjoy such pleasure, especially when my master (husband) is also so old?'

"Then the Lord said to Abraham, 'Why did Sarah laugh? Why did she say, Can an old woman like me have a baby? Is anything too hard for the Lord? I will return about this time next year, and Sarah will have a son.'

"Sarah was afraid, so she denied it, saying, 'I didn't laugh.' But the Lord said, 'No – you did laugh.'"

Like Abraham (Genesis 17:17), Sarah could not restrain laughter at the thought of bearing a child at her advance age. Confronted by the daily realities of her physical condition, she found it impossible to believe God's promise. But though she muffled her laughter and denied it when confronted, God knew of it. His rhetorical question – "Is anything too hard for the Lord" – was the ultimate rebuke of Sarah's unbelief and our own. The God who gave a child to aged Abraham and Sarah, the God who later caused a virgin to conceive, can do whatever He pleases.

This covenant made with Sarah promised certain blessings to her and her offspring,

Isaac, for many generations. It was in two parts:

1. Commands:
   A. Change her name from Sarai to Sarah, both meaning princess. (Genesis 17:15)
   B. Calling her son Isaac – meaning laughter (Genesis 17:19)

2. Promises:
   A. To be blessed with a son (Genesis 17:16-19; 18:10-15)
   B. To be made a mother of nations (Genesis 17:16)
   C. To become a mother of many kings (Genesis 17:16)
   D. Abrahamic covenant to be continued with Isaac (Genesis 17:19)
   E. Abrahamic covenant to be continued with Isaac's seed forever (Genesis 17:19).

When Abram was 99 years old, God came again to talk with him. This time He gave Abram the sign of circumcision, saying, "My covenant shall be in your flesh for an everlasting covenant" (Gen. 17:13).

During this same visitation, God changed Abram's and Sarai's names, putting the H in each of them, thus identifying them even more closely with Himself, for He was called in the Hebrew, Ya-weh (Gen. 17:5, 15).

86

Summary of the Abrahamic Covenant

When God established a covenant with Abraham, it was another dramatic turning point in human history. Abraham and his heirs (the nation of Israel) received an unconditional promise. Under this covenant, God promised to make Israel a great nation, to bless the seed of Abraham, to give him a great name, to make him a blessing, to bless those who blessed him and curse those who cursed him, to give him the promised land, and through his descendants to bless all the families of the earth with a Redeemer. Israel's failure in this dispensation was illustrated by their leaving the land to settle in Egypt, and resulted in bondage there. Israel's final testing under this dispensation occurred when God attempted to draw them back to the land. But they refused Him in unbelief at Kadesh-Barnea.

It is important to remember that God's promise to Abraham and his seed still hold true today, including, "I will bless them that bless you, and curse him that curses you; and in you shall all families of the earth be blessed. (Genesis 12:3).

In fulfillment of the first part of this verse, we have seen the decline and ruin of nations which have persecuted the Jews. On the other hand, there are examples of blessing on the countries which have dealt kindly with these chosen people. America is a prime example of being a blessed nation because we have been Israel's major friend and ally.

We do not have to probe ancient history for examples, for we have seen, after World War II, the trials of Germany which killed six million Jews under Hitler.

Our present government leaders are leading our nation away from supporting and blessing Israel. If this trend continues and we support the nations that are Israel's enemies, they will place America under the curse of God. America's Christians need to pray and vote and work for those leaders who will continue to bless God's ancient people.

CHAPTER VI

THE DISPENSATION OF LAW
(Exodus 14:22 – Matthew 3:17)
Length: Over 1,718 years

This dispensation is reckoned from the time of the Exodus from Egypt, led by Moses, to the coming of Christ as heralded by John the Baptist (Luke 16:16).

The length is deduced from the following information: 41 years between the time the children of Israel left Egypt and entered Canaan. From the time they entered the promised land until they asked for a king (the period of Joshua and the judges) was approximately 520 years.

The time from the reign of Saul to the deportation to Babylon accounts for more than 513 years. We know the Babylonian captivity lasted 70 years, and that the Medo-Persian kings to the restoration under Nehemiah added another 94 years.

From the restoration under Nehemiah to John's announcing the Lamb of God, was 480 years (see Daniel 9:25, which states that from the commandment to rebuild Jerusalem until "Messiah shall be cut off" shall be 69 weeks, or 483 years). John heralded Jesus about three years before His crucifixion, making the 480 years.

Someone has said that when God wants to do something in the world, He starts with a baby. So Moses was born for a task.

In the final years of the Dispensation of Promise, Moses, the key man for the next dispensation, was born. The Egyptian king ordered all newborn Hebrew boy babies had to be killed. This was one more attempt of Satan to thwart the promise that "the seed of the woman" should bruise his head. If he could destroy this nation which had sprung from the loins of Abraham, he could nullify the promises of God. However, Moses escaped the sentence of death in infancy, and was brought up in the palace of the Egyptian king.

Moses always identified with the Hebrew slaves. When he was grown, he knew that he was not an Egyptian. He was not the only child of Amram and Jochebed. There were at least two others – Miriam and Aaron. Miriam was used of God to preserve his life as an infant, for this baby had been born to do a big job.

When Moses was a grown man, he was groomed and trained to become a Pharaoh. One day he saw an Egyptian slave master brutally beating a Hebrew slave. He lost his temper and murdered the Egyptian. He buried the dead Egyptian, but, as usually happens at a crime scene, there were eye-witnesses and he was forced to flee for his life.

Moses escaped out into the desert to elude his Egyptian pursuers. He arrived in the land of Midian and married a priest's daughter. Her name was Zipporah. This story is told in Exodus 2:15-25.

To give you a little history lesson, Midian was a son of Abraham through Keturah (Genesis 25:1-6). The land of Midian was originally a part of the land of Cush, from which descended the Ethiopians, and was evidently under the domination of Ethiopia at that time. Numbers chapter 12 says that Zipporah was an Ethiopian. Years later Miriam, Moses' sister, was upset with Moses because his wife was an Ethiopian. Most Bible scholars believe that Zipporah was a black lady, and this was the cause of Miriam's anger.

So, God's man, who talked face to face with God, had a mixed racial marriage, which hadn't bothered God in the least. Also, KIng Solomon, David's son, had an affair with the Queen of Sheba from Ethiopia, who was a brilliant and beautiful black lady. They produced a son who is well known in Ethiopian history.

In Exodus 2:23-24, it says, "And the children of Israel sighed by reason of their bondage, and they cried, and their cry came up unto God . . . And God heard their groaning, and God remembered His covenant with Abraham, with Isaac, and with Jacob."

As a result, God went out to the desert where He had been preparing Moses, and called Moses from a burning bush. Again God referred to the promise and confirmed it to Moses (Exodus 3:6-8).

Moses went back to Egypt as he had left, a deliverer, but this time he was backed by the promises of God, and he was to succeed. In the process of delivering His people, God directed ten plagues against objects of worship or things sacred to the Egyptians, thereby causing these very things to become abominations to them.

Following the last plague, Pharaoh was at last, more than glad to let God's people go. In the deliverance of Israel on the night the death angel passed over, through the blood on the lintels and on the doorposts, we see the scarlet line of redemption, which began with the first animal sacrifice in the Garden of Eden. It is in evidence throughout the Old Testament, and climaxes with Christ's death at Calvary.

Each dispensation had begun with a special manifestation of God to certain persons – Adam, Noah, Abraham. This dispensation could, in a way, be said to have opened with a revelation of God to Moses at the burning bush. But it is still in its opening moments, when God reveals Himself to the whole nation of Israel.

The Healing Covenant

Exodus 15:26 (NLT) "He (Moses) said, 'If you will listen carefully to the voice of the Lord your God and do what is right in His sight, obeying His commands and keeping all His decrees, then I will not make you suffer any of the diseases I sent on the Egyptians; for I am the Lord who heals you' (Jehovah Rapha).

Here, God revealed Himself to the newly freed Israelites as Yahweh Rapha – "The Lord who heals." His promise to keep the Israelites free from disease was conditioned upon their continued repentance and obedience. Deuteronomy 29:5-6 makes it clear that God kept His word and preserved them during their journey. And the ministry of Jesus and the apostles continued to demonstrate that God has profound power over human suffering. Trust that even today God has the power to heal you of sickness.

Exodus 23:25-26 (NLT) "You must serve only the Lord your God. If you do, I will bless you with food and water, and I will protect you from illness. There will be no miscarriages or infertility in your land, and I will give you long full lives."

This covenant was made with Israel and all who desired or chose to come under the covenant of God as given to Moses. It was in two parts:

1. Commands:
   A. Diligently hearken to God's voice (Exodus 15:26; Leviticus 26:14-15)
   B. Do that which was right in His sight. (Exodus 15:26)
   C. Give ear to His commandments (Exodus 15:26)
   D. Keep all His statutes (Exodus 15:26; Leviticus 26:3, 14-15).
   E. Serve the Lord (Exodus 23:25)

2. Promises:
   A. "I will put none of these diseases upon you" (Exodus 15:26)
   B. "I am the Lord that heals you' (Exodus 15:26).
   C. "I will take away sickness from the midst of you" (Exodus 23:25).

This covenant was made a part of the new covenant, for Christ "took our infirmities and bare our sicknesses."
(Isaiah 53; Matthew 8:17; I Peter 2:24).

This brings us to Exodus Chapter 19. Quoting from the New Living Translation (NLT), let's begin quoting at Exodus 19:1.

"Exactly two months after the Israelites left Egypt, (Hebrew – "In the third month after the Israelites left Egypt, on the very day, i.e., two

lunar months to the day after leaving Egypt")
they arrived in the wilderness of Sinai. After
breaking camp at Rephidim, they came to the
wilderness of Sinai, and set up camp there at
the base of Mount Sinai."
This perhaps means the same day the third
month began, meaning the first day of the third
month – Sivan, or May.

Israel left Egypt on April 15th, on the Sabbath.
(see Numbers 33:3). It has been calculated
that it was exactly 50 days from the first
Passover when the Israelites left Egypt until
the Law was given at Sinai. So the Law was
originally given on the Day of Pentecost. They
started their journey from Rephidim, which was
called Rameses in Numbers 33:3, which was
the same as modern Cairo, Egypt.

The Exodus was the beginning of months (New
Year) for Israel's new calendar, corresponding
with the latter part of our Gregorian calendar,
March and the first part of April. Previously,
the old Jewish year began in September. It
was called the civil year, while this new
calendar was called the ecclesiastical year.

The Mosaic Covenant / Law / Sinaitic
Covenant
(Exodus 19:3-8)

Exodus 19:3-8 (NLT) "Then Moses climbed the
mountain to appear before God. The Lord
called to him from the mountain and said, 'Give

these instructions to the family of Jacob; announce it to the descendants of Israel: You have seen what I did to the Egyptians. You know how I carried you on eagles' wings (sustained you) and brought you to Myself. Now if you will obey me and keep My covenant, you will be My own special treasure from among all the peoples on earth; for all the earth belongs to Me. And you will be My kingdom of priests, My holy nation'. This is the message you must give to the people of Israel.

"So Moses returned from the mountain and called together the elders of the people and told them everything the Lord had commanded him. And all the people responded together, 'We will do everything the Lord has commanded'. So Moses brought the people's answer back to the Lord."

The leaders or elders of the people represented the entire nation. Their consent was counted as the consent of the entire nation and obligated the entire nation to keep the covenant the leaders had confirmed with God.

This was the same kind of representative form of government we have in America. Our representatives and leaders in Washington D.C., that we voted into office, make laws and decisions that obligate us. They are supposed to represent the will of the people, their constituents, but many times they ignore the wills of the majority and vote their own desires.

The leaders at Sinai said to Moses: "W are well able to perform what God commands." This was a statement of pride. In other words, they said, "It's a piece of cake; we can keep all of God's commands in our own strength".

So Moses reported what the leaders said to God, and God held the whole nation of Israel to their words.

Verse 8 was the change from the Abrahamic Covenant to the Sinaitic Covenant.... from God's grace to the Law.

The dispensation of Law meant government by the Mosaic Covenant. This covenant was given to Israel in order to reveal sin and death. The Law reflected the holiness of a personal God, instructed the people in God's discipline, reminded them through its priests and sacrifices of God's salvation, and acted as a pedagogue, or teacher, to lead them to Christ. The Law contained three elements: (1) commandments revealing the righteousness of God; (2) judgments expressing social requirements; and (3) ordinances directing the religious life of Israel. No one was ever saved by keeping the Law; it was simply God's moral guideline for Israel. This dispensation ended with vicarious judgment at the Cross, as Christ died for the sins of all humanity.

There was law in the earth before the giving of the Law that is usually identified with the Ten Commandments. Even in the dispensation of Innocence there was a law which Adam and

Eve failed to keep. There were laws of Human Government given to Noah, as recorded in Genesis 9. Even grace is mentioned in connection with Noah, for he "found grace in the eyes of the Lord", but this was not the fullness of grace. The fullness of the Law was by Moses, and the fullness of grace came by Jesus Christ (John 1:16).

The actual giving of the Law, including the Ten Commandments, came within the year of the exodus of Israel from Egypt under the leadership of Moses.

Israel under the Law

Israel accepted the Law. It was not forced upon them, yet having it in tables of stone, even hearing it from Moses while his face shone with the glory of God's presence, did not change their natures.

After 40 years of wandering in the wilderness, Israel entered the land of Canaan, promised to them through Abraham. But there were giants in the land; there were battles to be fought. When they compromised God's plan, they suffered. When they obeyed, they prospered. God kept His part of the covenant; they often failed, and when they failed they were punished.

There came a time when God used judges to rule over the people, and when they asked for a king, God let them have a king. Saul, David, and Solomon ruled in succession over a united kingdom for a total of 120 years. Then under the sons of Solomon, the kingdom was divided. Benjamin and Judah, from whose line the Messiah was to come, separated from the other ten tribes.

The two kingdoms still had a common destiny, even though they elected to go their own ways. Through prophets in both kingdoms, God reminded them of the Law and of the promised Messiah.

The rise and fall of the Gentile kingdoms around them affected the Jewish people, but only in the manner God allowed. For example, Daniel, who was of the kingdom of Judah, was taken captive along with many others when Nebuchadnezzar besieged Jerusalem. Daniel was brought to the attention of the king and given a high position in the government which had been used to chastise his own nation.

Daniel served under two Babylonian kings – Nebuchadnezzar and Belshazzar, and Darius the Mede and Cyrus the Persian. God had named Cyrus long before he was born (Isaiah 44:28-45:1) and designated him as a restorer of Jerusalem. This prophecy was fulfilled in the restoration of Jerusalem at the decree of Cyrus, under the direction of Ezra and Nehemiah (Ezra 1:1-3).

Following the time of Malachi, there were about 400 years of supposed "silence", so-called because we have no record that Israel had a prophet in this period. More of the people were colonists in Persia than were in the land God had promised to them. In fact, only a remnant of Judah and some priests and Levites lived in Palestine, which had been restored to them under Cyrus. Palestine was a buffer between Persia and Egypt, and suffered when these nations were at war.

Although the Israelites were supposedly without prophets in those years preceding the coming of Christ, they could at least see prophesy fulfilled. They had the writings of Daniel, and could watch as the image he had seen (Daniel 2) began to take shape. The Persian kingdom fell; then Syria, and Greece came to power. Under Grecian dominion, the land of Palestine was divided into the five provinces which are mentioned in the Gospels -- Galilee, Samaria, Judea, Trachonitis, and Perea.

Antiochus Epiphanes, the "little horn" of Daniel 8:9, foreshadowed many things that the Antichrist will do when he comes on the scene. Under Antiochus Epiphanes' rule, the Jews were hurt and humiliated as their temple was desecrated and they were forced to eat pork, which was an abomination to them.

This persecution brought the four Maccabean brothers to the forefront as they led a revolt against the Gentile rulers. The revolt resulted in civil war, which in turn, was interrupted by the coming of Rome to power and the conquest of Judea and Jerusalem.

The Mosaic Covenant was also called the Old Covenant or the Old Testament. (Exodus 20:1 – 24:8)

2 Corinthians 3:6-18 (NLT) "He (God) has enabled us to be ministers of His <u>New Covenant</u>. This is a covenant not of written laws, but of the Spirit. <u>The old written covenant ends in death; but under the new covenant, the Spirit gives life.</u>

"The old way, with laws etched in stone, led to death, though it began with such glory that the people of Israel could not bear to look at Moses' face. For his face shone with the glory of God, even though the brightness was already fading away. Shouldn't we expect far greater glory under the new way, now that the Holy Spirit is giving life? If the old way, which brings condemnation, was glorious, how much more glorious is the new way, which makes us right with God! In fact, that first glory was not glorious at all, compared with the overwhelming glory of the new way. So if the old way, which has been replaced, was glorious, how much more glorious is the new, which remains forever!

"Since this new way gives us such confidence, we can be very bold. We are not like Moses, who put a veil over his face so the people of Israel would not see the glory, even though it was destined to fade away. But the people's minds were hardened, and to this day, whenever the old covenant is being read, the same veil covers their minds so they cannot understand the truth. And this veil can be removed only by believing in Christ. Yes, even today when they read Moses' writings, their hearts are covered with that veil, and they do not understand.

"But whenever someone turns to the Lord, the veil is taken away. For the Lord is the Spirit, and wherever the Spirit of the Lord is, there is freedom. So all of us who have had that veil removed can see and reflect the glory of the Lord. And the Lord – who is the Spirit – makes us more and more like Him as we are changed into His glorious image."

In verses 7-11, is Paul saying that the Old Covenant was bad? At first glance, perhaps, it may seem he is, but look closer. The Old Covenant was from God and was His good gift to Israel, though it ultimately led to Israel's condemnation. Paul is clear that the Old Covenant was glorious (verse 9) even while it led to death. If this is true, then the New Covenant, which leads to life, must be much more glorious. In fact, 3:10 indicates that the difference is so great that the Old Covenant can even be considered "not glorious" in comparison.

When we read 2 Corinthians 3:12-16, we find out that Paul is not saying that reading the Old Testament is bad or that doing so hardens a Christian. Instead, Paul makes it clear that he is referring to those who read the Old Testament without believing in Christ. Trying to understand Moses' writings (the first five books of the Old Testament) without believing in Christ is like trying to read them while looking through a piece of cloth – one will not be able to clearly make out what it is truly saying. Reading the Law does harden the heart of those who do not believe in Christ. In Paul's thought, believing in Jesus Christ is the only way to correctly understand the Old Covenant.

In verses 17-18 in chapter 3, "For the Lord is the Spirit , and wherever the Spirit of the Lord is, there is freedom. So all of us who have had that veil removed can see and reflect the glory of the Lord. And the Lord –Who is the Spirit – makes us more and more like Him as we are changed into His glorious image."

As Paul discusses the New Covenant, he highlights the Spirit's role in transforming us. When we turn to the Lord, we receive the Holy Spirit in our hearts, and the Spirit begins transforming our lives, making us more and more like Jesus Christ. Are you a born-again Christian? If so, the Holy Spirit lives in you. You can leave your sins, because Jesus forgave them at the cross and gave you His righteousness. You can be transformed into a new person with new thoughts and a new life-style. You simply need to co-operate with the Holy Spirit. And where the Holy Spirit is, there is freedom – we are free from sin's guilt, we are being made free from its power over our day-to-day lives, and we look forward to the day when we will be free from even sin's presence.

The Levitic Covenant

Numbers 25:5-15 (NLT) "So Moses ordered Israel's judges,
'Each of you must put to death the men under your authority who have joined in worshiping Baal of Peor'."

"Just then one of the Israelite men brought a Midianite woman into his tent, right before the eyes of Moses and all the people, as everyone was weeping at the entrance of the Tabernacle. When Phinehas, son of Eleazer and grandson of Aaron, the priest, saw this, he jumped up and left the assembly. He took a spear, and rushed after the man into his tent. Phinehas thrust the spear all the way through the man's body and into the woman's stomach. So the plague against the Israelites was stopped, but not before 24,000 people had died.

"Then the Lord said to Moses, 'Phinehas, son of Eleazor and grandson of Aaron, the priest, has turned My anger away from the Israelites by being as zealous among them as I was. So I stopped destroying all Israel as I had intended to do in My zealous anger. Now tell him that I am making My special covenant of peace with him. In this covenant, I give him and his descendants a permanent right to the priesthood, for in his zeal for Me, his God, he purified the people of Israel, making them right with me.

"The Israelite man killed with the Midianite woman was named Zimri, son of Salu, the leader of a family from the tribe of Simeon. The woman's name was Cozbi; she was the daughter of Zur, the leader of a Midianite clan."

Phinehas defended God's holiness and so was promised a priestly line (which continued until the dissolution of the priesthood in the New Testament era). His execution of the sinful couple served as substitution (making atonement) for the sins of all the people.

This covenant was given through Moses to Phinehas, the son of Levi, who was zealous for the Lord, and executed judgment upon rebels. It consisted of two great promises:
1. Peace and blessing to Levi's house
2. An everlasting priesthood.

The Palestinian Covenant
Leviticus 26; Deuteronomy 11:8-32; 27:1-30:20

In Leviticus 26, God listed what the Israelites must do to receive His blessings – obey His commands. Moses also lists the punishment for disobedience.

God created people so that He could have a relationship with them, and they could delight in Him. He told the Israelites to make a tent (sanctuary, Tabernacle) so that He could live with them (Exodus 25:8). He wanted to be in their midst. In Leviticus 26:11-12, God said He would live among His people and walk with them. Throughout history, God has continually sought to have fellowship with humanity. So much did He want to be reconciled with His people – to have them live with Him eternally – that He was willing to send His Son to dwell with them on earth. John 1:14 says that "the Word (Jesus) became human and made His home among us." Through the person of Jesus, God took on a physical, human body, and came to walk among people.

What a loving God we have! He is not a distant deity whose back is turned to us, whose voice is never heard, or whose will is impossible to know. God wants to walk with us today, and live in us as the center of our affections and the goal of our energies. God loves us and, though He doesn't need it, finds our fellowship delightful, so much so, that His plan to rescue fallen creation includes restoring our relationship with Him. And one day, God's people will see Him as He is, and that one look will change us forever (1 John 3:2).

In Deuteronomy Chapter 11, God gave the Israelites a choice between a blessing and a curse, before they entered the Promised Land.

In Deuteronomy 27-30, we find a strong admonition to choose obedience and thus life. This is the final call to Israel to embrace the covenant with God.

This covenant was made with Israel through Moses, and was conditioned upon the obedience of the nation. There were seven parts:

1. Dispersion for disobedience
   Deuteronomy 28:63-68 (NLT) "Just as the Lord has found great pleasure in causing you to prosper and multiply, the Lord will find pleasure in destroying you.. You will be torn from the land you are about to enter and occupy. For the Lord will scatter you among all the nations from one end of the earth to the other. There you will worship foreign gods that neither you nor your ancestors have known, gods made of wood and stone! There, among those nations, you will find no peace or place to rest. And the Lord will cause your heart to tremble, your eyesight to fail, and your soul to despair. Your life will constantly hang in the balance. You will live night and day in fear, unsure if you will survive. In the morning you will say, 'If only it were night!' And in the evening you will say, 'If only it were morning!' For you will be terrified by the awful horrors you see around you. Then the Lord will send you

back to Egypt in ships, to a destination I promised you would never see again. There you will offer to sell yourselves to your enemies as slaves, but no one will buy you."

Deuteronomy 30:1 (NLT) "In the future, when you experience all these blessings and curses I have listed for you, and when you are living among the nations to which the Lord your God has exiled you, take to heart all   these instructions."

2. Repentance while in Dispersion
Deuteronomy 30:2 (NLT)"If at that time, you   and   your   children return to the Lord your God, and if you obey with all your heart and all your soul , all the commands I have given you today, then the Lord your God will restore your fortunes."

Zechariah 12:10-14 (NLT) "Then I will pour out a spirit of grace and prayer on the family of David and on the people of Jerusalem. They will look on   Me whom they have pierced and mourn for Him as for an only son. They   will grieve bitterly for Him as for a firstborn son who has died. The sorrow   and mourning in Jerusalem on that day, will be   like   the   great   mourning   for Hadad-rimmon in the Valley of Megiddo.

"All Israel will mourn, each clan by itself, and with the husbands separate   from their wives. The clan of David will mourn alone, as will the clan of Nathan, the clan of Levi, and the clan of Shimei. Each of the surviving clans from Judah will mourn separately, and with the husbands, separate from their wives."

"Hadad-rimmon" combines the names of two ancient storm deities. They shared worship space with Anat, the deceased consort of Baal, in a temple located near Megiddo. Canaanite fertility rituals required periodic mourning, and it is to these rituals that Zechariah referred, comparing their mourning to the grief in Jerusalem.

3. The Return of the Lord.
   Deuteronomy 30:3 (NLT) "Then the Lord your God will restore your fortunes. He will have mercy on you and gather you back from all the nations where He has scattered you."

   Acts 15:13-18 (NLT) "When they had finished, James stood and said, 'Brothers, listen to me. Peter has told you about the time God first visited the Gentiles to take from them a people for Himself. And this conversion of Gentiles is exactly what the prophets predicted. As it is written (Amos 9:11-12, Greek Version): 'Afterward, I will return and restore the fallen house of David. I will rebuild its ruins and restore it, so that the rest of humanity might seek the Lord, including the Gentiles – all those I have called to be mine. The Lord has spoken – He who made these things known so long ago.'"

Read Zechariah 14, which talks about the Lord's millennial rule of the earth. Zechariah described "the Day of the Lord" a time of ultimate blessing for God's people and ultimate judgment on God's enemies. Such images are common whenever the prophets describe "that day". These blessings and curses were fulfilled at various times in history, but ultimately they will be fulfilled when Jesus returns. The New Testament writers (especially John, in Revelation) describe Jesus' second coming with imagery drawn from Zechariah and the other prophets.

In verses 4-5, Zechariah described God's coming by saying His "feet" will touch the Mount of Olives in Jerusalem. God's coming will split the earth, making a way of escape for His persecuted flock. Earth-shaking images were often used to communicate the awesome power of God when He comes in judgment (see Psalm 18:7-12; Isaiah 29:5-7). This scene is similar to the imagery of Revelation 16:17-21, which describes God judging His enemies through an earthquake that splits the great city.

4. Restoration in the Land
Deuteronomy 30:5 (NLT) "The Lord your God will return you to the land that belonged to your ancestors, and you will possess that land again. Then He will make you even more prosperous and numerous than your ancestors!"

Isaiah 11:1-12 (NLT) "Out of the stump of David's family will grow a shoot – yes, a new Branch bearing fruit from the old root.
And the Spirit of the Lord will rest on Him – the Spirit of wisdom and understanding, the Spirit of counsel and might, the Spirit of knowledge and the fear of the Lord.
He will delight in obeying the Lord. He will not judge by appearance nor make a decision based on hearsay.
He will give justice to the poor and make fair decisions for the exploited. The earth will shake at the force of His word, and one breath from His mouth will destroy the wicked.
He will wear righteousness like a belt and truth like an undergarment.
In that day the wolf and the lamb will live together; the leopard will lie down with the baby goat. The calf and the yearling will be safe with the lion, and a little child will lead them all.

The cow will graze near the bear. The cub and the calf will lie down together. The lion will eat hay like a cow.

The baby will play safely near the hole of a cobra. Yes, a little child will put its hand in a nest of deadly snakes without harm.

Nothing will hurt or destroy in all My holy mountain, for as the waters fill the sea, so the earth will be filled with people who know the Lord.

In that day the heir to David's throne will be a banner of salvation to all the world. The nations will rally to Him, and the land where He lives will be a glorious place.

In that day the Lord will reach out His hand a second time to bring back the remnant of His people – those who remain in Assyria and northern Egypt; in southern Egypt, Ethiopia, and Elam; in Babylonia, Hamath, and all the distant coastlands.

He will raise a flag among the nations and assemble the exiles of Israel. He will gather the scattered people of Judah from the ends of the earth."

5. National conversion.

Deuteronomy 30:6 (NLT) "The Lord your God will change your heart and the hearts of all your descendants, so that you will love Him with all your heart and soul and so you may live!" (Also read Isaiah 66)

Romans 11:26-27 (NLT) "The One who rescues will come from Jerusalem, and He will turn Israel away from ungodliness. And this is My covenant with them, that I will take away their sins."

In Isaiah 66:3-4, it shows us that the Lord despises the religiosity of the unrepentant. Religious observance without sincerity of heart is the moral equivalent of paganism in God's eyes.

Verses 2(b) – 4) In the New Living Translation makes the above statement very plain. "I will bless those who have humble and contrite hearts, who tremble at My word.

But those who choose their own ways – delighting in their detestable sins – will not have their offerings accepted. When such people sacrifice a bull, it is no more acceptable than a human sacrifice. When they sacrifice a lamb, it's as though they had sacrificed a dog! When they bring an offering of grain, they might as well offer the blood of a pig. When they burn frankincense, it's as if they blessed an idol.

I will send them great trouble – all the things they feared. For when I called, they did not answer. When I spoke, they did not listen. They deliberately sinned before My very eyes and chose to do what they know I despise."

6. Judgment of Israel's oppressors

Deuteronomy 30:7 (NLT) "The Lord your God will inflict all these curses on your enemies and on those who hate and persecute you.

Matthew 25:45-46(NLT) "And He will answer, 'I tell you the truth, when you effused to help the least of these, My brothers and sisters, you were refusing to help me.'

And they will go away into eternal punishment, but the righteous will go into eternal life."

7. National prosperity

Deuteronomy 30:9-10 (NLT) "The Lord you God will then make you successful in everything you do. He will give you many children and numerous livestock, and He will cause your fields to produce abundant harvests, for the Lord will again delight in being good to you as He was to your ancestors. The Lord your God will delight in you if you obey His voice and keep the commands and decrees written in this Book of instruction, and If you turn to the Lord your God, with all your heart and soul."

Read Romans Chapter 11 and you will learn about God's mercy on Israel

(verses1-24). Verses 25-36 explain one
of God's mysteries —God's mercy is for
everyone!" Some of the people of Israel
have hard hearts, but this will last only
until the full number of Gentiles comes to
Christ. And so all Israel will be saved"
(verses 25(b)-26).

The Stump of David's Family

Romans 11:1 -Terrible tragedy can destroy
families. Particularly in ancient times, war or
famine could destroy entire generations or
even entire tribes. David's descendants
suffered greatly from the Assyrian and
Babylonian invasions; they were left lifeless
and hopeless as a stump. But eventually, God
raised up Jesus, who was in the line of David,
from this seemingly ruined family. God is also
able to raise up stable, godly leadership from
your family, too. What steps do you need to
take to clear the way for God to work in and
through your family? How can you train your
family to become humble leaders in the church
and the world?

Romans 11:2 – The reign of the coming son of
David would be ideal in every respect because
He would be empowered by the Spirit of the
Lord. Throughout the Old Testament, the Spirit
of the Lord came upon Israel's political,
military, and religious leaders in order to
empower them for particular tasks. But the
Holy Spirit would uniquely rest on this
descendant of David.

Jesus defends the poor and exploited (Romans 11:4). God's people have always known Him as a rescuer. God may work through kings and queens, but He takes special delight in lifting up the lowly. Isaiah prophesied that the future Messiah would focus His efforts on the lowest in society – the poor, the sick, and the children. God's ways have not changed. You should imitate Jesus by helping to change the lives of the downtrodden around you.

Verses 6-9 beautifully describe the harmony and peace that would characterize the reign of Jesus, our coming king. When Jesus reigns, there will no longer be violence or strife in the created order.

Nature will be at peace (verse 6). Isaiah prophesied of a time when nature will be at peace. Right now, all of creation is burdened under the curse of sin. Death reigns everywhere because of sin, and that includes all plants and animals. They suffer because of our sinfulness. But in that future time, all creation will be at rest, for the Messiah will reign over the earth. What a day that will be! Are you excited about seeing the earth restored to its former glory? Praise Jesus that He will return and do away with the curse that Adam brought upon creation.

Matthew 24:31 (NLT) "And He will send out His angels with the mighty blast of a trumpet, and they will gather His chosen ones from all over the world – from the farthest ends of the earth and heaven."

Jesus will return! When the head of state enters a hall for an official function, everyone knows it. Attention is drawn to him as he takes his proper seat, his presence is announced, and all in attendance are aware that the business at hand can now begin. That is what it will be like when Jesus returns. Whether every person on the planet will see it or not, is beside the point – no one will mistake this Person for another charlatan. Everyone who sees His arrival will know that life on earth will be forever altered. In that moment, our faith will instantly be converted to sight, for everything we have believed about Jesus will be finally and completely demonstrated as true. **GET READY FOR THAT DAY AS IF IT WERE TOMORROW!**

The Salt Covenant

Leviticus 2:13 (NLT) "Season all your grain offerings with salt to remind you of God's eternal covenant. Never forget to ad salt to your grain offerings."

Salt was also directly associated with God's covenants with Aaron and David. As a preservative, salt symbolized permanence.

Numbers 18:19 (NLT) "Yes, I am giving you all these holy offerings that the people of Israel bring to the Lord. They are for you and your sons and daughters, to be eaten as your permanent share. This is an eternal and unbreakable covenant between the Lord and you, and it also applies to your descendants."

The Hebrew word translated "covenant", literally means a "covenant of salt." A covenant made with Israel concerning the sacrifices they were to offer forever. Every sacrifice was offered with salt as a symbol of preservation.

In Palestine and surrounding countries, salt was used in making covenants; and if persons dined together on food with salt in it, they became friends, though they may have been enemies before. The Arab expression, "There is salt between us," or "He has eaten of my salt," means partaking of the hospitality which cements friendship. Covenants were generally confirmed at sacrificial meals, and salt was always present. The covenant of salt pictured the everlasting friendship between God and His people.

The Davidic Covenant

2 Samuel 7:1-17 (NLT) "When King David was settled in his palace and the Lord had given him rest from all the surrounding enemies, the king summoned Nathan the prophet. 'Look,' David said, 'I am living in a beautiful cedar palace, but the Ark of God is out there in a tent!'

"Nathan replied to the king, 'Go ahead and do whatever you have in mind, for the Lord is with you.'

"But that same night the Lord said to Nathan, 'Go and tell My servant David, this is what the Lord has declared: Are you the one to build a house for Me to live in? I have never lived in a house, from the day I brought the Israelites out of Egypt until this very day. I have always moved from one place to another with a tent and a Tabernacle as My dwelling. Yet, no matter where I have gone with the Israelites, I have never once complained to Israel's tribal leaders, the shepherds of My people Israel. I have never asked them, 'Why haven't you built Me a beautiful cedar house?'

"'Now go and say to My servant David, This is what the Lord of Heaven's Armies has declared: I took you from tending sheep in the pasture and selected you to be the leader of My people Israel. I have been with you wherever you have gone, and I have destroyed all your enemies before your eyes. Now I will make your name as famous as anyone who has ever lived on the earth! And I will provide a homeland for My people Israel, planting them in a secure place where they will never be disturbed. Evil nations won't oppress them as they've done in the past, starting from the time I appointed judges to rule My people Israel. And I will give you rest from all your enemies.

"'Furthermore, the Lord declares that He will make a house for you – a dynasty of kings! For when you die and are buried with your ancestors, I will raise up one of your descendants, your own offspring, and I will make his kingdom strong. He is the one who will build a house – a temple- for My name. And I will secure his royal throne forever. I will be his father, and he will be My son. If he sins, I will correct and discipline him with the rod, like any other father would do. But My favor will not be taken from him as I took it from Saul, whom I removed from your sight. Your house and your kingdom will continue before Me for all time, and your throne will be secure forever.'

"So Nathan went back to David, and told him everything the Lord had said in this vision."

David's lovely cedar and stone palace had been constructed for him as a goodwill gesture by King Hiram of Tyre (2 Samuel 5:11 (NLT) "Then King Hiram of Tyre sent messengers to David, along with cedar timber and carpenters and stonemasons, and they built David a palace."), a city on the Mediterranean coast northwest of Jerusalem. The contrast between the ornate palace in which David lived and the simple tent in which the Ark of the Covenant was being kept, made a strong impression on him. David believed the Ark, which represented God's throne and hence, God's Presence, should have a better home than it did.

Starting in 2005, Dr. Eilat Mazar of Hebrew University, has led a team of archaeologists in excavating around Jerusalem, and discovered King David's palace at the summit of Mount Zion, just north of the ancient walled part of the city. After one season of digging, she discovered a massive wall up to 10 feet wide in some places, and running 100 feet long, east to west.

The following digging season, Dr. Mazar expanded the dig site, discovering a much larger wall over 16 feet wide, testifying of the building's importance and grandeur. As she put it, this was "not just a house, but a fantastic house." A house – you could say – fit for the king of a mighty nation.

Dr. Mazar believes that only 20 percent of the palace has been uncovered. Plans are underway for further excavation in 2013 and beyond.

In 2 Samuel 7:3-7, we read that David asked the prophet Nathan whether he should build a Temple for God, and Nathan gave the go-ahead. But God then intervened. Though He praised David for his desire to build a Temple (! Kings 8:18), He rejected the plan for two reasons. First, God had not asked for a Temple. That did not mean that a Temple could never be built; God simply did not want one built yet. Second, David was not the man for the job. He was a warrior who had shed much blood (1 Chronicles 22:8-9), and the construction of the Temple would be accomplished by a "man of peace" – David's son, Solomon, who would rule in the era of peace that David had won by the sword. Until then, God was content to dwell in a tent, as His people had lived in tents for so long.

To ease David's disappointment over not being allowed to build the Temple, God first reminded him of past grace – that God had raised David up from tending sheep to ruling Israel, that He had been with David through all of his struggles, and that He had destroyed all of David's enemies.

Then He promised continuing grace – that He would make David's name famous through all the earth. God also promised that the line of Solomon, the son of David --- and hence, David's line – would last forever. There was only one way this promise could be fulfilled – one of David's descendants would be the Messiah, who would reign forever. For this reason, the angel Gabriel told Mary that God would give her son the throne of his ancestor, David. And He will reign over Israel forever; His Kingdom will never end!" (Luke 1:32-33).

This agreement was made with David and his house through Nathan the prophet, and was conditioned upon obedience, as all other covenants. It was to be an everlasting covenant, containing 7 blessings:

1. A Davidic house forever. Psalm 89:20-37 (NLT) "I have found My servant David. I have anointed him with My holy oil. I will

steady him with My hand; with My powerful arm I will make him strong.

"His enemies will not defeat him, nor will the wicked overpower him. I will beat down his adversaries before him and destroy those who hate him.

"My faithfulness and unfailing love will be with him, and by My authority he will grow in power. I will extend his rule over the sea, his dominion over the rivers. And he will call out to Me, 'You are my Father, my God, and the Rock of my salvation.'

"I will make him My firstborn son, the mightiest king on earth. I will love him and be kind to him forever; My covenant with him will never end.

"I will preserve an heir for him; his throne will be as endless as the days of heaven.

"But if his descendants forsake My instructions and fail to obey My regulations, if they do not obey My decrees and fail to keep My commands, then I will punish their sin with the rod, and their disobedience with beating.

"But I will never stop loving him nor fail to keep My promise to him. No, I will not break My covenant ; I will not take back a single word I said.

"I have sworn an oath to David, and in My holiness I cannot lie; his dynasty will go on forever; his kingdom will endure as the sun. It will be as eternal as the moon, My faithful witness in the sky!"

Luke 1:32-35 (NLT) "He (Jesus) will be very great and will be called the Son of the Most High. The Lord God will give him the throne of his ancestor David. And he will reign over Israel forever; His Kingdom will never end!

"Mary asked the angel, 'But how can this happen? I am a virgin.'

"The angel replied, 'The holy Spirit will come upon you, and the power of the Most High will overshadow you". So the baby to be born will be holy, and He will be called the Son of God."

2. A Davidic throne forever. Isaiah 9:6-7 (NLT) "For a child is born to us, a Son is given to us. The Government will rest on His shoulders. And He will be called: Wonderful Counselor, Mighty God, Everlasting Father, Prince of Peace.

"His government and its peace will never end. He will rule with fairness and justice from the throne of His ancestor David for all eternity. .The passionate commitment of the Lord of Heaven's Armies will make this happen!"

The promises of a new age were intimately connected to the birth of an heir of David, who would firmly establish God's eternal kingdom. The titles given to this son of David follow a logical sequence from the planning of a battle to the securing of victory. "Wonderful Counselor" suggests a brilliant strategist, "Mighty God" is literally "God is a warrior" in the Hebrew Text; "Everlasting Father" was a common royal title in the ancient Near East; and "Prince of Peace suggests the kind of reign the Davidic king would enjoy. Isaiah's hope was realized in the birth of Jesus Christ.

3. A Davidic kingdom forever. (The same Scriptures as in Numbers 1 and 2).

4. A sure land for Israel Forever. Genesis 17:8 (NLT) "And I will give the entire land of Canaan where you now live as a foreigner, to you and your descendants. It will be their possession forever, and I will be their God."

    2 Samuel 7:10 (NLT) "And I will provide a homeland for My people Israel, planting them in a secure place where they will never be disturbed. Evil nations won't oppress them as they've done in the past."

5. No more affliction from the nations forever. Deuteronomy 28:7 (NLT) "The Lord will conquer your enemies when they attack you. They will attack you from one

direction, but they will scatter from you in seven!"

This blessing from God was conditional upon Israel's obedience to God's commands.

6. The Fatherly care of God forever.. 2 Samuel 7:14 (NLT) "I will be his father, and He will be My son. If He sins, I will correct and discipline him with the rod, like any father would do."

2 Corinthians 6:15-18 (NLT) "What harmony can there be between Christ and the devil? How can a believer be a partner with an unbeliever? And what union can there be between God's temple and idols? For we are the temple of the living God.

"As God said: 'I will live in them and walk among them. I will be their God, and they will be My people. Therefore, come out from among unbelievers, and separate yourselves from them', says the Lord.

'Don't touch their filthy things, and I will welcome you. And I will be your Father, and you will be My sons and daughters, says the Lord Almighty.'"

We are God's temple. Although God is Everywhere, He was present in the Temple in a unique way, during the time of the Old Testament. Without that presence, the Temple was just another building.

The exciting news of the New Covenant is that now we are God's temple – God's Spirit now manifests itself in our lives, makes us Holy, and therefore, Paul reasoned, the Corinthians were to honor God with their temple–bodies by pursuing sexual purity and unit with one another. Their bodies were to be used as implements of worship.

Since God lives inside us through the Holy Spirit, we are empowered to overcome addictions, temptations, and sin. Without the Holy Spirit in us, the best we can do is cope with sin. But with God, we can stop coping and cooperating with sin, and start eradicating it. With the truth of the gospel and by the power of the Holy Spirit, we can overcome sin.

In verses 16-18, Paul supports his point from the Old Testament. Phrases from Exodus 25:8; Leviticus 26:11-12; Isaiah 52:11; Ezekel 37:27; and Hosea 1:10 merge into a single quotation, a style of argument familiar among Jewish writers. These quotations serve as a promise. Paul argues that Christians should not respond by binding themselves to unbelievers. Doing so will inevitably harm their own moral purity.

7. An eternal covenant. 2 Samuel 7:10-16; Isaiah 9:6-7; and Luke 1:32-33 prove his point, as we have seen before.

The Relationship of Law and Grace

Obviously, it would take volumes of books to discuss every reference in the Bible which would shed light on this very important subject. However, the following references are given to show the purpose of the Law in the light of God's total program; the relationship of Law and Grace; and the relationship of the child of God under Grace to the dispensation of Law.

One function of the Law was to define the sin that was already in the world. Paul expresses this in Galatians 3:19 (NLT) "Why, then, was the Law given? It was given alongside the Promise to show people their sins. But the Law was designed to last only until the coming of the Child (Jesus) who was promised."

The Law revealed what God already knew, but it had to be proved to man – that man is a sinner and he cannot be good of his own accord.

Since the Law can neither save (Galatians 3:10-14) nor can it annul the Abrahamic Covenant (Galatians 3:15-18), what purpose did it serve? It was added (alongside the Covenant) because of transgressions, that is, to reveal the hideous character of man's sin. Transgression was subsequent, not prior to, the Law. The Law laid down the divine standard, and when man overstepped it, he became guilty of transgression. The inferiority of the Law to the Abrahamic Covenant is seen in three ways:

1. The Law "was added" after the Covenant and thus was subordinate to it.
2. The Law was temporary, being in effect only "till the seed (Jesus) should come".
3. Unlike the Covenant God gave directly to Abraham, the Law was ordained (handed down) indirectly by God through angels to its mediator, Moses. (See Acts 7:53).

The Law proved that knowing what to do is not enough; man must also have a change of heart that makes him want to do what he knows is right. "Let me put it another way. The Law was our guardian (schoolmaster) until Christ came; it protected us until we could be made right with God through faith. And now that the way of faith has come, we no longer need the Law as our guardian (schoolmaster)." (Galatians 3:24-25 NLT).

In antiquity the schoolmaster was a family slave who led a boy to and from school, overseeing his conduct. In like manner, the Law pointed out our sin and led us to Christ, Who alone can put away sin. After one's conversion to Christ, he is no longer under the curse of the Law, as it has fulfilled its divinely intended purpose. The Law has been fulfilled in Jesus!

John 1:17 (KJV) says, "For the Law was given by Moses, but Grace and Truth came by Jesus Christ." Grace is a Person! Law was given, Grace came!

Let's read 1 Corinthians 15:56 (KJV) "The sting of death is sin; and <u>the strength of sin is the Law.</u>" Paul declares that the strength of sin is the Law. The more you are under the Law, the more sin is strengthened!

Romans 6:14 is a WOW! Verse. (NLT) "Sin is no longer your master, for you no longer live under the requirements of the Law. Instead, you live under the freedom of God's Grace." Liberty is not license! The believer is not free to do whatever he wants. He is free only to do that which is consistent with the character of God. True freedom is freedom from sin. Christians are under grace, the Spirit's law. The more grace you receive, the more power you have to over- come sin.

Another verse worth quoting is Matthew 11:28-30 (NLT). "Then Jesus said, 'Come to me, all of you who are weary and carry heavy burdens, and I will give you rest. Take my yoke upon you. Let Me teach you, because I am humble and gentle at heart, and you will find rest for your souls. For my yoke is easy to bear, and the burden I give you is light.'"

Under Law, the yoke is hard and heavy. The burden is on you to perform. The yoke of Grace is easy and light because it involves none of you and all of Christ.

The Law was as a bud. Grace is the full flower. Certain parts that are apparently very important when a flower is in the bud stage, yield their place of prominence when the blossom unfolds. So the Law with its legalism moves into the background with the unfolding of the Grace of God in Jesus Christ. "For what the Law could not do in that it was weak through the flesh, God, sending His own Son in the likeness of sinful flesh and for sin, condemned sin in the flesh: that the righteousness of the Law might be fulfilled in us who walk not after the flesh, but after the Spirit" (Romans 8:3-4).

Even if it were possible to keep the whole Law, we cannot be justified by it. We are "justified by faith." The Dispensation of Law ended with the most ironic action by mankind in all history – the crucifixion of Jesus. Thus, by seeking to rid the world of the Son of God, Jews and Gentiles shared together in closing the Dispensation of Law and the opening the door of Grace to whosoever will.

CHAPTER VII

THE DISPENSATION OF GRACE

Matthew 4:1 – Revelation 19-21
Length: From the Birth of Christ
To the Second Coming of Christ

This Dispensation has already lasted over 2,000 years. It will not end until after the Rapture of the Church and the fulfillment of Revelation 4:1 – 19:10.

We are now living in the Dispensation of Grace, which has already lasted longer than any of the preceding dispensations. We speak of this as the Dispensation of Grace because the fullness of God's grace has been manifested in the life, death, and resurrection of Christ. Since this dispensation personally concerns everyone living today, I will deal with its provisions and blessings in more detail than those covered in previous dispensations.

John 1:17 "For the Law was given by Moses, but Grace and Truth came by Jesus Christ." Grace is a person! Grace is God's love and unmerited favor to all humanity through Jesus Christ. Grace is the predominant characteristic of this age. "If you have heard of the dispensation of the grace of God which is given me for you. . . "(Ephesians 3:2)

Dispensations and Covenants

People must recognize the relationship between a dispensation and a covenant if they would understand God's plan and objective throughout the ages. A dispensation is an administration within a period of time that is based on a conditional test to determine if people will be faithful to God and His conditions. A covenant is an eternal agreement made by God with humanity, revealing what God will do for people individually or collectively. God made covenants with the human race throughout history that specifically relate to one of the seven dispensations. Each covenant reveals principles in embryonic form by which God will relate to humanity.

Man can choose to reject the covenant or principles of God, and will, to some extent, in every dispensation. When he violates the covenant, man suffers the consequences in the form of a judgment, bringing that dispensation to an abrupt end. While all Christians recognize at least two dispensations –Law and Grace – there are seven major dispensations and their covenants.

Just as God had given some laws to mankind before the Dispensation of Law, so His grace was manifested in many ways to man before the Dispensation of Grace began. Each of the previous dispensations began with a demonstration of God's favor, or grace. For instance, we see God's grace manifested even in the Antediluvian period. "Noah found grace in the eyes of the Lord" (Genesis 6:8). See other examples in Genesis 19:19; Exodus 33:12-17; 34:9; Psalm 84:11; Proverbs 3:34. The word "grace" appears 38 times in the Old Testament. Grace literally means "unmerited love and favor" granted to unworthy sinners who are unable to help themselves.

In this Age of Grace, man is permitted to approach God "by a new and living way, which He has consecrated for us, through the veil, that is to say, His flesh" (Hebrews 10:20). Jesus Christ is the "new and living way" by which believers have direct access into the very Holy Place of God.

The New Living Translation (NLT) puts it this way: "By His death, Jesus opened a new and life-giving way through the curtain into the Most Holy Place."

In the Old Testament Tabernacle and Temple, a curtain set off the Most Holy Place. Only the High Priest was allowed to enter, and then only once a year on the Day of Atonement. When Jesus died on the cross, the curtain was torn in two. This signified that in Christ, believers are invited into God's most holy Presence to fellowship with Him.

We are no longer restricted, as men were under the Law, to offering the "blood of bulls and goats, and the ashes of a heifer."

Christ, "by His own blood entered in once into the holy place, having obtained eternal redemption for us . . . And for this cause He is the mediator of the New Testament, that by means of death, for the redemption of the transgressions that were under the first testament, they which are called might receive the promise of eternal inheritance" (Hebrews 9:11-15).

Hebrews 9:9-15 (NLT) "This is an illustration pointing to the present time. For the gifts and sacrifices that the priests offer are not able to cleanse the consciences of the people who bring them. For that old system deals only with food and drink and various cleansing ceremonies – physical regulations that were in effect only until a better system could be established.

"So Christ has now become the High Priest over all the good things that have come. He has entered that greater, more perfect Tabernacle in heaven, which was not made by human hands and is not part of this created world. With His own blood – not the blood of goats and calves – He entered the Most Holy Place once for all time and secured our redemption forever.

"Under the old system, the blood of goats and bulls and the ashes of a young cow could cleanse people's bodies from ceremonial impurity. Just think how much more the blood of Christ will purify our consciences from sinful deeds so that we can worship the living God. For by the power of the eternal Spirit, Christ offered Himself to God as a perfect sacrifice for our sins. That is why He is the One who mediates a new covenant between God and people; so that all who are called can receive the eternal inheritance God has promised them. For Christ died to set them free from the penalty of the sins they have committed under that first covenant."

The Old Testament sacrifices might be compared to the writing of a check. The paper on which it is written is practically worthless. Yet it is used and accepted in place of money, since it is backed by what has been deposited in the bank. Christ's death was deposited from the foundation of the world as that which backed the Old Testament sacrifices. With Christ's death on the cross, the deposit was released and all the past checks were honored and paid.

That the Dispensation of Grace supersedes the Dispensation of Law may be seen throughout the New Testament, but nowhere is it explained in more detail than in the letter to the Hebrews, Chapter 10, verses 8-10, summarizes it clearly: (NLT) "First, Christ said, 'You did not want animal sacrifices or sin offerings or burnt offerings or other offerings for sin, nor were You pleased with them' (though they are required by the Law of Moses). Then He said, 'Look, I have come to do Your will.' He cancels the first covenant in order to put the second into effect. For God's will was for us to be made holy by the sacrifice of the body of Jesus Christ, once for all time."

Because the will of God which Christ came to establish included the manifestation of God's grace to every person, "This High Priest of ours understands our weaknesses, for He faced all of the same testings we do, yet He did not sin. So let us come boldly to the throne of our gracious God. There we will receive His mercy, and we will find grace to help us when we need it most." (Hebrews 4:15-16).

Was Jesus able to yield to temptation? I believe that He was able to yield. Satan sure thought Jesus was able to yield. That's why he tried so hard to get Him to yield. He was able to yield, but He would not. For our sakes He would not sin and cut off our only means of salvation. Jesus defeated Satan by quoting Scripture to him. We also can defeat Satan by using the same method.

Have you heard the saying, "There's no such thing as a free lunch"? While this proverb may be true in everyday life, it is not so with God. The writer of Hebrews makes sure his readers know that God's grace and mercy are there for the asking – all we have to do is declare our need. Our High Priest, Jesus, understands our plight and has access to the Father's Presence, encouraging us to approach God's throne boldly. There we will receive mercy (release from deserved punishment) and grace (undeserved favor). Do you come boldly, admitting your deepest needs to God? Come without fear and admit your need for God's mercy and grace.

Under the Law, which had a "shadow of good things to come", the priests stood "daily ministering and often offering the same sacrifices, which can never take away sins: but this man (Jesus), after He had offered <u>one sacrifice</u> for sins forever, sat down at the right hand of God." (Hebrews 10:11-12)

Under the Old Covenant the priest's work was never done; he remained standing (there were no seats available in the temple) always in God's Presence, mediating for the people. But Christ has finished the work and sat down. This profound action fulfills Psalm 110:1, where God invites His Messiah to sit at His side.

Man in Old Testament times was saved by looking <u>forward</u> to what was to be accomplished, and offered up sacrifices in faith. Since the cross, in the Dispensation of Grace, man looks <u>back</u> to the cross and is saved by accepting what has been accomplished there already.

"There is one God, and one mediator (go between) between God and men, the Man Christ Jesus; who gave Himself a ransom for all" (1Timothy 2:5-6). When Christ died on Calvary, He paid the sin debt for all those Old Testament saints who died in faith, as well as for all those who should afterward believe on Him.

Man had miserably failed under each of the preceding dispensations, and now last of all, God sent His Son into the world to die for man's sin and to redeem man back to God. "God was in Christ, reconciling the world unto Himself" (2 Corinthians 5:19). Christ's work was a "once-for-all-time work; "There remains no more sacrifice for sin."

God has made this salvation available to everyone, without restriction, Jew and Gentile, yet the receiving of its blessings and benefits hinges upon each person's acceptance of Jesus Christ as His own personal Savior (Mark 16:15-16; John 1:12).

The acceptance or rejection of Jesus Christ as the only Savior constitutes the primary test during this present dispensation. "For the grace of God that brings salvation has appeared to all men" (Titus 2:11).

This salvation is all-inclusive, covering all sin of all peoples of all times. No sin is too small but what it demands a covering. "Without the shedding of blood there is no remission." No sin is too large but what the blood sacrifice of Christ will cover it. All people, from the remote to the renown, the down-and-outers and the up-and-outers, must have the same blood covering for their sins, from Adam to our time, and through the Millennium; all need to plunge into this fountain opened in the House of David for sin and uncleanness.

Man's sin and shame and God's redeeming grace are the sum and substance of the Bible. As man's iniquity is unfathomable, so is God's Grace: "Where sin abounded, grace did much more abound" (Romans 5:20). We praise God that the divine plan of redemption reaches the lowest sinner, and lifts the believer into a life of victory, happiness, holiness and eternal bliss. His grace extends to man's spirit, soul and body, and even to nature, which came under the curse of sin (Genesis 3:7-19; Romans 8:19-23).

The New Covenant

Matthew 26:28 (NLT) ". . . for this is <u>My blood, which confirms the covenant between God and His people</u>. It is poured out as a sacrifice to forgive the sins of many."

In this passage, Jesus explained the New Covenant in the context of the Passover feast to bridge the connection between the Old and New Covenant.

2 Corinthians 3:16-18 (NLT) "But whenever someone turns to the Lord, the veil is taken away. For the Lord is the Spirit, and wherever the Spirit of the Lord is, there is freedom. So all of us, who have had that veil removed can see and reflect the glory of the Lord. And the Lord – who is the Spirit – makes us more and more like Him as we are changed into His glorious image."

As Paul discusses the New Covenant, he highlights the Holy Spirit's role in transforming us. When we turn to the Lord, we receive the Holy Spirit in our hearts, and the Spirit begins transforming our lives, making us more and more like Jesus Christ. Are you a born-again Christian? If so, the Holy Spirit lives in you. You can leave your sins, you can be transformed. You do not need some additional power or some particular prayer. You simply need to cooperate with the Holy Spirit. And where the Holy Spirit is, there is freedom – we are free from sin's guilt; we are being made free from its power.

Hebrews 8:6 (NLT) "But now Jesus, our High Priest, has been given a ministry that is far superior to the old priesthood, for He is the One who mediates for us a far better covenant with God, based on better promises."

The writer makes a difficult point for his Jewish audience: there is a better covenant based on better promises than those of the Old Testament.

This is the covenant made by Jesus. It is still in force, and includes all the terms, conditions, commands, promises and benefits revealed in the 27 books of the New Testament.

The reason the new covenant excels the old is that the old was only for a time, a place – Palestine, and a people – the Jews. The new covenant is for all time, all lands, and all people.

The 10 commandments, in particular, were abolished, along with the whole law of Moses. In Acts, chapter 15, we read about the first doctrinal controversy in the first century church. This controversy was settled in Acts 15, but despite that, many Christians, then as now, were drawn away from the simple Christian faith by the "law" fallacy. The whole church at Galatia went back under the law, and was condemned by Paul. Even Peter, Barnabas, and others were carried away with this false doctrine for a while.

The law of Moses has been abolished and done away (2 Corinthians 3:6-15); cast out (Galatians 4:21-31); abolished (Ephesians 2:15); blotted out; taken out of the way (Colossians 2:14-17); changed (Hebrews 7:12); disannulled (Hebrews 7:18); replaced; has vanished (Hebrews 8:6-13 and 10:9).

The entire law was abolished, but 9 of the 10 were re-instated in the new covenant. Keeping the Sabbath (the fourth commandment) is the only one that was not re-instated into the new covenant.

The Founding of the Church

At the beginning of the Age of Grace, Christ started the Church as a called-out people to follow Him.

We have often stated that the Church was born on the Day of Pentecost. In one sense that is true, because 3,000 people answered Peter's altar call, which resulted in a large group of believers who formed the first major congregation.

Actually when Jesus had gathered His first believers about Him, He had started the New Testament Church. So there was already a large body of believers who followed Him before His crucifixion. It was not a perfect church, just as today's church is not perfect. But it was a Church – an ECCLESIA – an assembly of called–out ones, even before Pentecost.

Let's listen in on a private conversation that Jesus had with some of His disciples. Fortunately it was recorded for us in Matthew 16:15-18 (NLT). "Then He asked them, 'But who do you say I am'" Simon Peter answered, 'You are the Messiah, the Son of the living God.' Jesus replied, 'you are blessed, son of Jonah, because My Father in heaven has revealed this to you. You did not learn this from any human being. Now, I say to you that you are Petros (Greek), Kephas (Aramaic), and upon this rock (petras) I will build My Church, and all the powers of hell will not conquer it.'"

Petros means a fragment of a rock or a small pebble. Jesus said He was Petras, an immovable stone. Christ Himself is the only foundation of His Church. Peter was only one of the builders.

What makes the Church what it is? Rules and bylaws? Denominational affiliation? Jesus didn't build a building and endow a fund or start a denomination – He invited people to know Him. Peter saw this; that is why he confessed that Jesus was 'the Messiah, the Son of the living God." It is that confession – the confident belief in Jesus as Lord – that is the foundation for the Church Jesus seeks to build.

"Church" is a New Testament word, first used by Christ here in Matthew 16:18. Christ was the first to announce the building of the New Testament Church, which is composed of both Jews and Gentile believers.

The Apostle Paul said in 1 Corinthians 10:31-33, "So whether you eat or drink, or whatever you do, do it all for the glory of God. Don't give offense to <u>Jews or Gentiles or the Church of God</u>. I, too, try to please everyone in everything I do. I don't just do what is best for me; I do what is best for others so that many may be saved."

The Rapture of the Church

The Dispensation of Grace will be fast coming to a close with the Rapture of the Church, a sudden and thrilling event for which we look with great anticipation.

The Rapture of the Church and the Second Advent of our Lord are confused by some as referring to the same event. However, this is cleared up as we remember that the Rapture occurs when the Lord comes in the clouds for His saints (all the righteous dead from Adam to our present day are raised), and we are caught up to meet the Lord in the air.

Paul, describing the Rapture prophetically in 1 Thessalonians 4:16-17, says: "For the Lord Himself shall descend from heaven with a shout, with the voice of the archangel, and with the trump of God: and the dead in Christ shall rise first: then we, who are alive and remain, shall be caught up together with them in the clouds, to meet the Lord in the air: and so shall we ever be with the Lord."

The Second Advent is the return of our Lord with His saints, to appear personally on the earth. Between the Rapture and the Second Advent, there is an interval of at least seven years, during which time the Old Testament saints and the Church are judged in heaven, and the Marriage Supper of the Lamb takes place.

Much of the confusion concerning the Rapture and the Second Coming is the result of the citing of the Second Advent Scriptures when preaching on the Rapture and vice versa. This should not be done unless the speaker makes it clear he is taking the Scripture out of its context. The context of the Scripture itself will make clear which event the writer intended.

For the benefit of everyone, I am listing the following Scriptures that deal with the Rapture:

Luke 21:34-36 (NLT): "Watch out! Don't let your hearts be dulled by carousing and drunkenness, and by the worries of this life. Don't let that day catch you unaware, like a trap. For that day will come upon everyone living on the earth. Keep alert at all times. And pray that you might be strong enough to escape these coming horrors and stand before the Son of Man."

The timing of some of the events in Chapter 21 are difficult to understand. Some of these details seem to have occurred sooner (21:31), others have been happening throughout history (21:25-26), and still others have not yet occurred (21:27). Luke summarizes what our response should be to Jesus' messages about the end times: **KEEP ALERT!** (21:36).

John 14:1-3 (NLT) "Don't let your hearts be troubled. Trust in God, and trust also in Me. There is more than enough room in My Father's home. If this were not so, would I have told you that I am going to prepare a place for you? When everything is ready, I will come and get you, so that you will always be with Me where I am."

The King James Version says: "In My Father's house are many mansions . . ." The New Living Translation refers to our eternal home as a room in our Father's home. The Greek word is OIKIA, which means "a dwelling place." The Father's dwelling place is heaven. The word "house" in verse 2, is "MONE" in Greek, which means "abiding places" or "abode". Also, in verse 2 it says, (KJV) "I go to prepare a <u>place</u> for you." The word translated "place" is from the Greek word TOPOS, which means "a place of habitation, such as a city".

Scripture describes heaven as a beautiful city where the redeemed will live for eternity. The glories of heaven belong only to those who have personally trusted Christ for their salvation.

Verse 3 refers to the Rapture, not the Second Advent. At this time, He will receive to Himself all the dead and living in Christ, who will come back to earth with Him at the Second Advent. Since Christ is in heaven, that is where we are to go at the Rapture.

<u>1 Corinthians 15:15-58:</u>   This is a fabulous study for everyone, and will answer many of the questions people have about death and life after this life.   However, we will only write verses 48-53, which pertain to the Rapture.

<u>15:48-53</u> (NLT): "Earthly people are like the earthly man, and heavenly people are like the heavenly man. Just as we are now like the earthly man, we will some day be like the heavenly man.

"What I am saying, dear brothers and sisters, is that our physical bodies cannot inherit the Kingdom of God. These dying bodies cannot inherit what will last forever.

"But let me reveal to you a wonderful secret. We will not all die, but we will all be transformed! It will happen in a <u>moment, in the blink of an eye</u>, when the last trumpet is blown. For when the trumpet sounds, those who have died will be raised to live forever. And we who are living will also be transformed. For our dying bodies must be transformed into bodies that will never die; our mortal bodies must be transformed into immortal bodies."

This is one of Paul's revelations—all will not die physically, but some will be changed to the likeness of those who do die. The living will be changed from mortality to immortality as quickly as the dead will be raised to immortality. The time needed for this is but a moment, in the twinkling of any eye. The Greek says, EN ATOMO, in an atom of time – a nano-second.

It will happen at the last of two trumpets which will sound at this time. At the first trumpet, the dead will be raised to immortality. At the second or last trumpet, the living will be changed to immortality and be caught up with the dead to meet the Lord in the air.

Here Paul focuses on the difference between our current bodies and our coming resurrection bodies. By referring to our resurrection bodies as "spiritual", Paul does not mean that they will be incorporeal. Instead, they will be like Christ's body, fully able to live forever in the age to come. Christ is, and will forever, remain both God and man, fully (and physically) human and also fully God – two distinct natures in one body.

2 Corinthians 5:1-9 (NLT) "For we know that when this earthly tent we live in is taken down (that is, when we die and leave this earthly body), we will have a house in heaven, an eternal body made for us by God Himself and not by human hands. We grow weary in our present bodies, and we long to put on our heavenly bodies like new clothing. For we will put on heavenly bodies (during the Rapture); we will not be spirits without bodies. While we live in these earthly bodies, we groan and sigh, but it's not that we want to die, and get rid of these bodies that clothe us. Rather, we want to put on our new bodies so that these dying bodies will be swallowed up by life. God Himself has prepared us for this, and as a guarantee, He has given us His Holy Spirit.

"So we are always confident, even though we know that as long as we live in these bodies we are not at home with the Lord. For we live by believing and not by seeing. Yes, we are fully confident, and we would rather be away from these earthly bodies, for them we will be at home with the Lord. So, whether we are here in this body or away from this body, our goal is to please Him."

Many ancient philosophers and religions argued that the physical world was inherently evil, and that eventually would be removed. On the contrary, Paul tells the Corinthians, the Christian's destination does not involve an eternal separation of body and soul. Instead, the Christian looks forward to a new, perfect body, with only a temporary separation of body and soul.

Paul views the Holy Spirit as the guarantee of the promise of a new body. The new body is yet to come, part of the promise of the new heavens and new earth, in which God will dwell with His people. The Holy Spirit is a down payment on that future time, a piece of it given to believers now. As God, in the Person of the Holy Spirit, is with us now, we can have confidence that God will fully be with us in the future.

So God has given us the earnest, or the first fruit of the Spirit, as a guarantee that we will be resurrected and put on immortality. While we live in the body, we are in our temporary home and absent from the eternal home with the Lord.

Verse 9 tells us that to die and be absent from the body means we go to heaven to be with the Lord. This is proof that the inner man does not go to the grave at death, but to heaven if one is righteous. If one is wicked, he goes to hell awaiting the resurrection of his body to stand before God at the Great White Throne Judgment. Those people did not accept Jesus as their Savior, so will be cast into the Lake of Fire for all of eternity (See Revelation 20:11-15).

Ephesians 5:25-27 (NLT) ". . . as Christ loved the Church, He gave up His life for her to make her holy and clean, washed by the cleansing of God's word. He did this to present her to Himself as a glorious church without a spot or wrinkle or any other blemish. Instead, she will be holy and without fault."

The Church is now glorious because of the glorious Gospel of Grace, the glorious power of God working in it to make it pure, holy, spotless, and without blemish. It will be presented to Christ, a glorious church at the Marriage Supper of the Lamb, and the glorious bodies that saints will receive during the Rapture.

Philippians 3:21 (NLT) "He (Jesus) will take our weak mortal bodies and (during the Rapture) change them into glorious bodies like His own, using the same power with which He will bring everything under His control."

When Jesus returns for His people, He shall change our vile (humble) body. The word "change" denotes external change – our "humble" bodies will undergo an outward transformation, without destruction of individuality. Our new bodies will be fashioned (conformed) or made like unto His glorious body. The word "fashioned" denotes internal change – we will experience an inward transformation of nature, as God makes us, in character, perfectly like His Son. That power by which God is able even to subdue all things (i.e., the universe) to Himself, is the same power that will be used to transform believers. This will all happen in a nano-second (twinkling of an eye). WOW!

1 Thessalonians 2:19-20 (NLT) "After all, what gives us hope and joy, and what will be our proud reward and crown, as we stand before our Lord Jesus when He returns? It is you! Yes, you are our pride and joy."

Finis Jennings Dake, in Dake's Annotated Reference Bible, gives the following comments concerning 1Thessalonians 2:19: Rapture and Second Advent

"This refers to the Rapture, not the Second Advent of Christ.

"These two comings should not be confused. The Scriptures that apply to one do not apply to the other. Not one passage refers to both events as if they were one. These two distinct comings are separated by several years, and so, are not two stages or phases of one coming.

"The Rapture is the first of the two comings, not a coming to earth but in the air. It could not be the second advent because Christ does not come to the earth to live here and fulfill a mission as He did at the first advent. When Christ meets the saints in the air, He takes them back to heaven with Him, and presents them before the Father's throne where they remain during the time the tribulation is running its course on the earth. (1 Thessalonians 3:13;

John 14:1-3). Christ does not remain in the air with the saints when they meet Him as in 1 Thessalonians 4:13-17. The marriage supper and the judgment of saints take place in heaven, then at the second advent, after the tribulation, Christ and the saints leave heaven together to come down to the earth (2 Corinthians 5:10; Revelation 19). The Rapture is the time Christ comes for the saints to take them to heaven.

"The Second Advent is the time He comes to the earth to live here and fulfill a mission. This is the time He comes from heaven with the saints, having raptured them at least 7 years before. The Second Advent cannot take place until all of Revelation 1:1-19:21 is fulfilled, while the Rapture can take place any moment without anything being fulfilled."

1 Thessalonians 4:15-17 (NLT) "We tell you this directly from the Lord: We who are still living when the Lord returns, will not meet Him ahead of those who have died. For the Lord Himself will come down from heaven with a commanding shout, with the voice of the archangel, and with the trumpet call of God. First, the Christians who have died, will rise from their graves. Then, together with them, we who are still alive and remain on the earth will be caught up in the clouds to meet the Lord in the air. Then we will be with the Lord forever."

The order of events at the time of Christ's coming is clearly given: (1) the Lord will descend with a shout, accompanied by the voice of the archangels, and the trump of God (1 Corinthians 15:52); (2) the dead in Christ will be resurrected; and (3) then those remaining will be caught up with them in the clouds. Dead in Christ is a technical expression for believers of the church age. Caught up (Greek: HARPAZO, means "to seize", "snatch"). The Latin word for carry off is RAPTUS, from which we get Rapture.

Although the word Rapture does not occur in the English Bible (the Latin Bible uses the verb Raptus from which Rapture derives), the idea is expressed in the words "caught up". The Rapture is the first phase of Christ's return, involving every Christian alive at that time. These Christians will be caught up to meet Him in the clouds, instantaneously receiving glorified bodies. All those who have died "in Christ" will be resurrected; those who are alive and saved at the time of the Rapture, will be caught up with Christ before the start of the "Seventieth Week of Daniel", that is ,the Great Tribulation.

A close examination of the prophetic Scriptures reveals a distinction between the Rapture (which relates to the Church) and the revelation of Christ in power and glory (which relates more to Israel).

James 5:7-8 (NLT) "dear brothers and sisters, be patient as you wait for the Lord's return. Consider the farmers who patiently wait for the rains in the fall and in the spring. They eagerly look for the valuable harvest to ripen. You, too, must be patient. Take courage, for the coming of the Lord is near."

Deuteronomy 11:14: The early and latter rains in Palestine, the early rain at seed time and the latter rain at harvest time, are used here to picture the fruit of the harvest of souls. The early rain fell in October, to moisten the parched soil and prepare it for sowing; the latter rain fell in March, to bring the crops to maturity.

The early spiritual rain fell at the founding of the Church (Acts 2:1-16) and the latter rain will be poured out at the end of this age, when the complete harvest of this Church Age will be gathered. As you wait for the Rapture, be patient. In the fullness of time (in God's timing), Jesus will be sent by the Father to gather us all to our eternal home.

1 John 2:28 (KJV) "And now, little children, abide in Him; that, when He shall appear, we may have confidence, and not be ashamed before Him at His coming.

This coming refers to the Rapture when Christ will come for the saints, who will rise to meet Him in the air.

We have to abide in Jesus. We live in Him and He lives in us. Sometimes we like to abide in Him, then we wake up to actualities, self-interest arises and the abiding is passed. There should be no condition of life in which we cannot abide in Jesus. If we continually remain grafted into Him, and our bodies are always the temples of the Holy Spirit, we will not be ashamed of our lifestyles at the time of the Rapture.

1 John 3:1-3 (NLT) "See how very much our Father loves us, for He calls us His children, and that is what we are! But the people who belong to this world don't recognize that we are God's children, because they don't know Him. Dear friends, we are already God's children, but He has not yet shown us what we will be like when Christ appears. But we do know that we will be like Him, for we will see Him as He really is. And all who have this eager expectation will keep themselves pure, just as He is pure."

At the Rapture when Christ comes to gather His followers, we will be transformed into His likeness. We will then have the same resurrection body that Jesus now has. This process has been working in us since the time that we accepted Christ as our Savior.

When the Rapture transpires, the saints will forever be free from all that hurts and all that decays. There will be no more sorrow, no more weeping, no more pain of any kind. We shall be in a land of eternal life, peace and joy, far away from the troubles of a sinful world, where all will receive their rewards according to their works. One good look at Him will a thousand sacrifices repay. His "well done, my child, you are welcome home," will more than repay us for any persecution or problems we received for serving Him in this life.

Here on earth, the Dispensation of Grace comes to a close as the others have – in God's judgment upon rebellious, disobedient man. Seven years of tribulation, "Such as was not, since the beginning of the world to this time, no, nor ever shall be," will follow the Rapture of the Church.

The tribulation will be seven years long (Daniel 9:27). It is known to Bible students as Daniel's seventieth week. It is primarily a time when God deals with Israel, bringing them back to Himself so that He might fulfill His covenant with them. It is a time of Jacob's trouble (Jeremiah 30:3-11), (not the church's trouble, for the church will have been raptured before this time).

The Antichrist will not be revealed until after the Rapture (2 Thessalonians 2:7-8). At the beginning of the seven-year period, he will make a covenant with the Jews, and he will break it after three and a half years. At the end of the seven year period, he will come against Israel.

At this point, the Lord Jesus will return to earth with His saints, to fight against and overcome the Beast and False Prophet at the Battle of Armageddon.

This great battle ends the era of Human Government, which began with Noah, and ushers in the final Dispensation, The Reign of Christ on Earth.

CHAPTER VIII

OVERVIEW OF REVELATION

GLIMPSE OF THE TRUTHS IN JOHN'S REVELATION

In order to touch on the Dispensational aspects of the prophecies in the Book of Revelation, I am including this brief overview.

Recognition of the three divisions of the Revelation is basic to understanding it. Revelation 1:19 lists the three divisions of the book. .

(NLT) "Write down what you have seen – both the things that are now happening and the things that will happen." Or, what you have seen and what they mean – the things that have already begun to happen.

1. "What you have seen." John was to write about his vision of Christ in the midst of the candlesticks (Revelation 1). And he wrote a vivid description of Jesus' physical features.
2. Things that are now happening." The things concerning the seven local churches that existed in John's day which he wrote about in Revelation chapters 2-3. However, since we are still in the Church Age,

they are applicable to us, both individually and prophetically.

3. "Things that will happen." This referred to the things that transpire after the Rapture of the Church (Revelation 4:1): ". . . Come up here, and I will show you what must happen after this." Referring to the things that transpire after the Rapture of the Church. From this verse on through the Revelation, the Church is no longer seen on earth, but in heaven, represented by the enthroned elders.

4. Chapter 4 – Deals with worship in heaven. It tries to put into human language what John saw – God's brilliance and opulence and majestic appearance. It talks about the 24 elders, representative of the Old and New Testament saints; the four living creatures before the throne; and the worship of these elders and creatures because of God's great creation.

5. Chapter 5 – This vision continues, but here our Lord is worshiped as Redeemer. The Lamb is the only person found worthy to open the seven-sealed scroll or book.

Revelation 6:1-8:1 concerns the opening of the seals. This is the beginning of the Great Tribulation and the rise of the Antichrist to power. The wrath that begins to be poured out upon the earth will continue for seven years, ending at the return of Christ to the earth (chapter 19).

The following seven events mark the opening of the seals:
1. The white horse rider signals the rise of the Antichrist after the Rapture of the Church. The white horse rider represents Conquest.

   Revelation 6:1-2 (NLT) "As I watched, the Lamb broke the first of the seven seals on the scroll. Then I heard one of the four living beings say with a voice like thunder, "COME!" I looked up and saw a white horse standing there. Its rider carried a bow, and a crown was placed on his head. He rode out to win many battles and gain the victory."

   Daniel 7:8, 24 (NLT) "As I was looking at the horns, suddenly another small horn appeared among them. Three of the first horns were torn out by the toots to make room for it. This little horn had eyes like human eyes and a mouth that was boasting arrogantly (vs. 24). .Its ten horns are ten kings who will rule that empire. Then another king will arise, different from the other ten, who will subdue three of them."

   Daniel 11:36-45 (NLT) "The king will do as he pleases, exalting himself and claiming to be greater than every god, even blaspheming the God of gods. He

161

will succeed, but only until the time of wrath is completed. For what has been determined will surely take place. He will have no respect for the gods of his ancestors, or for the god loved by women, or for any other god, for he will boast that he is greater than them all. Instead of these, he will worship the god of fortresses – a god his ancestors never knew – and lavish on him gold, silver, precious stones, and expensive gifts. Claiming this foreign god's help, he will attack the strongest fortresses. He will honor those who submit to him, appointing them to positions of authority and dividing the land among them as their reward.

"Then at the time of the end, the king of the south will attack the king of the north. The king of the north will storm out with chariots, charioteers, and a vast navy. He will invade various lands and sweep through them like a flood. He will enter the glorious land of Israel, and many nations will fall, but Moab, Edom, and the best part of Ammon will escape. He will conquer many countries, and even Egypt will not escape. He will gain control over the gold, silver, and treasures of Egypt, and the Libyans and Ethiopians will be his servants.

"But then news from the east and the north will alarm him, and he will set out in great anger to destroy and obliterate many. He will stop between the glorious Holy mountain and the sea and will pitch his royal tents. But while he is there, his time will suddenly run out, and no one will help him."

2 Thessalonians 2:7-8 (NLT) "For this lawlessness is already at work secretly, and it will remain secret until the one who is holding it back steps out of the way. Then the man of lawlessness will be revealed, but the Lord Jesus will kill him with the breath of His mouth and destroy him by the splendor of His coming."

2. The red horse rider takes peace from the earth and brings war. Of course, the red horse rider represents War.

   Revelation 6:3-4 (NLT) "When the Lamb broke the second seal, I heard the second living being say, 'Come!' Then another horse appeared, a red one. Its rider was given a mighty sword and the authority to take peace from the earth. And there was war and slaughter everywhere."

3. The black horse rider ushers in famine because he represents famine.

   Revelation 6:5-6 (NLT) "When the Lamb broke the third seal, I heard the third living being say, 'Come!' I looked up and saw a black horse, and its rider was holding a pair of scales in his hand. And I heard a voice from among the four living beings say, 'A loaf of wheat bread or three loaves of barley will cost a day's pay.' "And don't waste the olive oil and wine.'"

Ezekiel 4:10-17 (NLT) "Ration this out to yourself, eight ounces of food for each day, and eat it at set times. Then measure out a jar of water for each day, and drink it at set times. Prepare and eat this food as you would barley cakes. While all the people are watching, bake it over a fire using dried human dung as fuel and then eat the bread. Then the Lord said, 'This is how Israel will eat defiled bread in the Gentile lands to which I will banish them!'

Then I said, "O Sovereign Lord, must I be defiled by using human dung? For I have never been defiled before. From the time I was a child until now I have never eaten any animal that died of sickness or was killed by other animals. I have never eaten any meat forbidden by the Law.'

'All right' the Lord said. 'You may bake your bread with cow dung instead of human dung.' Then He told me, 'Son of man, I will make food very scarce in Jerusalem. It will be weighed out with great care and eaten fearfully. The water will be rationed out drop by drop, and the people will drink it with dismay. Lacking food and water, people will look at one another in terror, and they will waste away under their punishment."

4. The pale horse rider brings pestilences – death and hell are with him. He represents Death.

   Revelation 6:7-8 (NLT) "When the Lamb broke the fourth seal, I heard the fourth living being say, 'Come!' I looked up and saw a horse whose color was pale green. Its rider was named Death, and his companion was the Grave. These two were given authority over one-fourth of the earth, to kill with the sword and famine and disease and wild animals. Jesus said that these troubles will precede the cosmic cataclysm in which God will destroy the ruling powers of evil (Mark 13:6-8).

5. We get a glimpse of the first tribulation martyrs (Revelation 6:9-11; 7:9-17; 15:2-4; 20:4)

6. The beginning of the wrath of God is announced (Revelation 6:12-17). It continues to be poured out in the trumpet and vial judgments.

7. There is silence in heaven (Revelation 8:1)

Chapter 7 – is parenthetical and is inserted for explanatory purposes. The events are not necessarily fulfilled at this time. The first event is the withholding of wrath until the servants of God are sealed in their foreheads. These 144,000, of all the tribes of Israel, are sealed and protected through the trumpet judgments. They are raptured in Revelation 12:5. The next we see of the 144,000 they are in heaven (14:1-5).

Revelation 7:9-17 shows the great multitude of Gentile believers who were saved and came out of the Great Tribulation. (NLT) "After this I saw a vast crowd, too great to count, from every nation and tribe and people and language, standing in front of the throne and before the Lamb. They were clothed in white robes and held palm branches in their hands. And they were shouting with a mighty shout, 'Salvation comes from our God who sits on the throne and from the Lamb!'

"And all the angels were standing around the throne and around the elders and the four living beings. And they fell before the throne with their faces to the ground and worshiped God. They sang,

"Amen! Blessing and glory and wisdom and thanksgiving and honor and power and strength belong to our God forever and ever! Amen.'

"Then one of the twenty-four elders asked me, 'Who are these who are clothed in white? Where did they come from?' And I said to him, 'Sir, you are the one who knows.' Then he said to me, '<u>These are the ones who died in the great tribulation.</u> They have washed their robes in the blood of the Lamb and made them white.

"That is why they stand in front of God's throne and serve Him day and night in His Temple. And He who sits on the throne will give them shelter.

They will never again be hungry or thirsty; they will never be scorched by the heat of the sun. For the Lamb on the throne will be their Shepherd. He will lead them to springs of life-giving water. And God will wipe every tear from their eyes.'"

Chapter 8 begins the seven trumpets that follow the seven seals in consecutive order: 1. vegetation destroyed (vs.7); 2. sea becomes blood (vs.8-9); 3. water is made bitter (vs. 10-11); 4. plants affected (vs.12-17); 5. demon locusts-the first woe (9:1-12); 6. demon horsemen-the second woe (9:13-21); 7. the casting out of Satan-the third woe (11:14-13:18).

All the events of Chapters 12 and 13 are fulfilled following the seventh trumpet, which blows in the middle of the week. The seven seals and seven trumpets signal 14 consecutive events which will be fulfilled in the order in which they are given, from the beginning to the middle of the week. The trumpet judgments as well as the wrath of God in the sixth seal are literal judgments as plainly described. There is a period of three and a half years from the seventh trumpet (11:1-3; 12:6,14; 13:5). The first trumpets must be fulfilled before this, and , if the seals are broken before the trumpets, all the seals and trumpets must be fulfilled before the middle of the week, or during the first three and a half years.

Chapter 10 is parenthetical, showing the Mighty Angel, which is Christ (Daniel 12:6), who announces the delay of time should be no longer, but that the Mystery of God should be finished.

The dominion of the Gentiles over the Jews is fast approaching the end. Only three and a half years are left, so at this time God dispatches two witnesses to the earth in the middle of the Great Tribulation, to prophesy and turn people to God (Revelation 11).

It is definitely stated in Malachi 4:4-5, that Elijah will be one of the witnesses.

Malachi 4:4-5 (LT) "Remember to obey the Law of Moses, My servant – all the decrees and regulations that I gave him on Mount Sinai for all Israel.

"Look, I am sending you the prophet Elijah before the great and dreadful day of the Lord arrives."

John the Baptist preached in the "spirit and power of Elijah," but could not be Elijah in person. See. . .

Luke 1:17 (NLT) "He (John the Baptist) <u>will be a man with the spirit and power of Elijah.</u> He will prepare the people for the coming of the Lord. He will turn the hearts of the fathers to their children, and he will cause those who are rebellious to accept the wisdom of the godly."

John 1:19-23 (NLT) "This was John's testimony when the Jewish leaders sent priests and Temple assistants from Jerusalem to ask John, 'Who are you?' He came right out and said, 'I am not the Messiah.'

"'Well then, who are you?' <u>they asked.</u> <u>'Are you Elijah?'</u> <u>'No,'</u> <u>he replied.</u>
'Are you the prophet we are expecting?' 'No.'

'Then who are you? We need an answer for those who sent us. What do you have to say about yourself?'

"John replied in the words of the prophet Isaiah: (Isaiah 40:3) 'I am a voice shouting in the wilderness. Clear the way for the Lord's coming!'"

So John will not be one of the witnesses. Elijah, himself, will return to the earth from heaven shortly before the coming of the great and dreadful day of the Lord. At that time there will be one of the greatest spiritual awakenings in the history of mankind. The hearts of fathers and sons, all children and parents, will be turned toward one another; families will be united in Christ; the Holy Spirit will be outpoured upon all flesh and even all of Israel will be saved as a result of the ministry of Elijah and the other witness.

The question still remains to be answered. Who is the other witness? Some believe the witnesses will be Elijah and Moses. Because both of them appeared at the transfiguration of Christ, they will also be the two witnesses. Of these two, only Moses would have already fulfilled Hebrews 9:27. ". . .it is appointed unto men once to die, but after this the judgment." Elijah never died before he was translated into heaven. There is only one other man who went to heaven without first dying. That man was Enoch.

Dake gives Scriptural evidence that the two witnesses will be Enoch and Elijah.

"They both were already in heaven when Zechariah prophesied, about 500 years before Christ (Zechariah 4:11-14)

"John saw them in heaven about 96 A.D., so whoever they are, they are two men translated to reside in heaven at least 500 years before Christ.

"When the 1,260 day ministry is finished, the supernatural angelic spirit out of the abyss will use the human Antichrist to kill them (Revelation 11:7).

"Since it is appointed unto men once to die;, it is certain that they are two men who have never died, so that they can die at the hands of the Antichrist in the future. This excludes Moses or any other man who has already died as one of the witnesses.

"They will remain dead for 31/2 days and then be resurrected (Revelation 11:8-11). This further proves that they are two men who have never died and that they will not be resurrected. Immortal men when they come from heaven to begin their ministry.

"There would seem to be only two men in the Bible who could fulfill these facts about the two witnesses. They are Enoch and Elijah. That Elijah will be one of them is clearly predicted in Malachi 4:5-6. John the Baptist was never Elijah, fulfilling this prophecy. He said that he was not Elijah, in John 1:21. He only came in the same spirit and power of Elijah, to prepare the hearts of men for the Messiah's first advent in the way that Elijah will prepare their hearts for the second coming of the Messiah.

"Enoch is the only other man translated that he should not see death in his lifetime on earth (Genesis 5:21-24; Hebrews 11:5; 2 Kings 2). Both must come back and die their own appointed death on earth, as all men must who live before the Rapture (Hebrews 9:27; I Corinthians 15:51- 58

171

"If either Enoch or Elijah had been translated in immortal, glorified bodies, they would have been the first-fruits of the resurrection instead of Christ.(1 Corinthians 15:20-23). This proves they are in heaven in their natural bodies. They will continue there until their return to fulfill Revelation 11: The lives of Enoch and Elijah are parallel in every sense, so their cases rise or fall together as to being the two witnesses."

Chapter 12 – Here we see the sun-clothed woman, symbolic of national Israel. Israel is foretold as a married woman who is bringing forth a "man child" (Isaiah 54:1-6; 66:7-8; Daniel 12:1). The Church has been raptured three and a half years before this event, and is never referred to as bringing forth a "man child." Neither are the Gentiles.

The man child symbolizes the 144,000 Jews who were sealed, in Revelation 7, raptured in Revelation 12:15, and seen in heaven on Mount Zion with the Lamb (Revelation 14:1).

Chapter 13 – Pictures two beasts. The first beast rises out of the sea, which is symbolic of Antichrist rising out from among the people.

We need to highlight the major prophesies of Daniel here, to understand the origin and identity of the Antichrist.

CHAPTER IX

MAJOR PROPHECIES OF DANIEL CONCERNING ANTICHRIST

The Book of Daniel consists of 12 Chapters, 357 verses, and 11,606 words. It is small, but important. We should never allow Satan to inject the thought into our minds that this is a hard or difficult book to be understood. The Bible is a book of marvelous unity. Any part of it will stand the test of comparison with other parts, with fuller understanding as the result. Daniel is no exception.

Daniel 2

The details and background leading up to Daniel's showing Nebuchadnezzar, the Babylonian king, his dream and interpretation, are found in Daniel 2:1-30. Daniel states the prophetic dream in verses 30-35, and gives the interpretation in the next ten verses.

Nebuchadnezzar's dream concerning a glittering image composed of five different materials. Its head was of fine gold (Babylonian Empire); its breast of silver (Medo-Persia); its belly and thighs of brass (Greece); and its legs of iron (Roman Empire). Its feet were part of iron and part of clay (Revised Roman Empire).

The Stone (Christ), cut out of the mountain without hands, struck the feet of the image and shattered it. Its fragments were blown away, but the Stone grew into a mountain, and filled the whole earth.

The same prophecy is repeated in Daniel 7, with the nations pictured as ferocious beasts. This is because Daniel 7 shows prophecy from God's standpoint, while in Daniel 2 it was viewed from the human standpoint.

In Daniel 7, the lion symbolizes Babylon, which was the head of gold on the image. The wings of this beast were plucked, representing the declining power of Babylon. A man's heart given to it shows the restoration of Nebuchadnezzar's right mind, and his return to the throne (Daniel 4). The bear in 7:5, symbolizes Medo-Persia, corresponding to the silver in the image. The three ribs symbolize the conquest of Lydia, Babylon, and Egypt by Medo-Persia. The leopard in 7:6, represents Greece, as does the brass in the image. The four heads are the four divisions of the empire which followed the death of Alexander.

The "diverse" beast described in 7:8, 20, and 24, symbolizes Rome, which was the iron in the image. The ten horns are the ten kings that will rule over the kingdoms formed out of the old Roman Empire, and the Little Horn is the Antichrist.

174

Daniel 8:1-26

In this chapter, Daniel narrows the origin of the Antichrist down to the four divisions of the Grecian Empire. These are four of the ten horns on the Beast in Daniel 7:24..

The ram in Daniel 8:1-4 symbolizes the Medo-Persian Empire, as is proved in verse 20. This is the same as the silver in the image (chapter 2) and the bear of Daniel 7:5.

The he-goat in Daniel 8:5, symbolizes the Grecian Empire, and is the same as the brass in the image and the leopard of Daniel 7:6.

The horn between his eyes that was broken off was the first king (8:21). This was Alexander the Great. When the horn was broken (Alexander died), four stood up, but not in Alexander's power.

In other words, Alexander died, and his kingdom was divided among his four generals. These became Greece, Turkey, Syria, and Egypt. Daniel 8:9 makes it clear that the Antichrist will come out of one of these four nations.

Daniel's Seventy Weeks
Daniel 9

Daniel's vision of the "seventy weeks" that was determined on his people (the Jews) and the

175

city of Jerusalem, revealed six events to take place during this 490 year period:

1) "to finish the transgression";
2) "to make an end of sins";
3) "to make reconciliation for iniquity";
4) "to bring in everlasting righteousness";
5) "to seal up the vision and prophecy," i.e., make an end of them by fulfillment of prophecies concerning Israel and Jerusalem;
6) "to anoint the Most Holy." This refers to the cleansing of the Holy of Holies, the temple and the city of Jerusalem, from the Abomination of Desolation and the sacrilege of the Gentiles under Antichrist, and to the establishment and anointing of the Millennial Temple of Ezekiel 40:46 and Zechariah 6:12-13.

The visions of Ezekiel chapters 40-48 concern things in the Millennium immediately following the regathering of Israel (chapter 37), and the Battle of Armageddon (chapters 38-39). These millennial conditions will continue in the New Earth period and throughout all eternity.

Starting with Chapter 40, the Millennial Temple sanctuary and oblations are described. In Zechariah 6, it tells us the Messiah will build the millennial temple and be a priest-king in it, of which Joshua and the restoration temple were only types.

These 490 years are divided into three periods. The first consisted of 49 years during which time the Holy City, street and walls, were to be built (Nehemiah 4: Daniel 9:25).

The second period consisted of 434 years. It began immediately after the restoration of the city and continued without a break to the time when the Messiah was "cut off" (or crucified) (Daniel 9:26).

The first periods covered 483 years, from the third decree to rebuild the city to the crucifixion of the Messiah. This accounts for 69 of the weeks of years, leaving the seventieth week (seven years) yet in the future, when God will again deal with Israel as a nation.

Daniel 11.

Michael, the archangel, gave a very detailed vision to Daniel. History confirms the accuracy of this vision. In Daniel 11:1-34, is recorded the history of Egypt, Syria, Greece and Turkey, from Darius to the future Antichrist.

In this study, we will learn from what country the Antichrist comes. Now we will weave Daniel's prophecy with history to see the foreknowledge of God in action.

In verse 3, the "mighty king" is Alexander the Great, King of Greece, who was so successful that in 13 years he completely destroyed the Medo-Persian Empire. At age 33, Alexander was at the height of his power as a dictator, when he died from alcoholism. Alexander the Great carried out the plans of his father, Philip of Macedon, to invade the Persian Empire (present day Iraq). The war began in 336 B.C., when Alexander came to the throne of Greece and Macedon. He only had 35,000 soldiers and $75,000 to start the war with, while the Persian king had a yearly revenue of $11,000,000, many millions in the treasury, and hundreds of thousands of soldiers, besides a great Navy. He had fully 50,000 Greek soldiers (mercenaries) hired with Greek generals. But in 13 years, Alexander conquered the whole Persian Empire and beyond. However when he died, his Grecian Empire was broken up into four divisions.

Alexander's four Generals were each made a king of one of the four divisions of the Grecian Empire. Ptolemy Lagidae was made the king of the South (Egypt). Seleucus I became the king of the North (Syria, Babylon and Media). Cassander took Greece, Macedon and the western parts of the empire. Lysimachus took Asia Minor, or present Turkey and Thrace.

Seleucus controlled the modern countries of Syria, Lebanon, Iraq and Iran. Each of these four generals wanted to be Alexander's successors, and control the whole Grecian Empire, so started trying to conquer each other.

Alexander's posterity was a threat, so they were all killed. Alexander's son by Roxane, became of age to take the throne. In 311 B.C., the child and his mother were murdered. In 15 years, not one of Alexander's family, including

3 wives, 2 sons, his brother and wife, and mother, was left alive.

Verse 5 mentions Ptolemy I, the king of the South (Egypt), who became strong, and added Cyprus, Phoenicia, Caria and Corinth to the kingdom of Egypt.

Ptolemy I was the son of Lagus, Macedonian nobleman of Eordaea, one of Alexander's trusted generals, and among his 7 bodyguards. Ptolemy I played a principle part in Alexander's campaigns in Afghanistan and India. His first occupation of Palestine was in 318 B.C. He left there in 315 B.C., due to a war with Antigonus. In 312 B.C., he and Seleucus, the fugitive satrap of Babylonia, invaded Palestine and defeated Antigonus at Gaza.

Again, Ptolemy I occupied Palestine and again, a few months later, he had to leave because his general lost another battle and Antigonus then entered Syria in force. He also lost Cyprus at this time. In 306-305 B.C., Antigonus invaded Egypt, but was defeated. In 302 BC Ptolemy I joined in a coalition in a war against Antigonus. He invaded Palestine a third time. On the report that Antigonus had won a great victory against Lysimachus in Asia Minor, he left Palestine again. But when he learned Antigonus was defeated in 301 B.C. by Lysimachus and Seleucus, he enterd Palestine a fourth time. The other members of the coalition had decided to give Palestine to Seleucus because they considered Ptolemy had deserted the coalition; and so, for the next 150 years, the Seleucid and Ptolemaic dynasties fought over Palestine. Ptolemy I died in 283 B.C., leaving a strong realm after 50 years of wars.

Also, in verse 5 it says, "one (of Ptolemy's) princes; . . . shall be strong above him, and have dominion." This was Seleucus I, called Nicator, the Conqueror, founder of the Seleucid Empire, 312 – 280 B.C. He lost out to Antigonus, who conquered Babylonia in 316 B.C. Seleucus fled to Egypt and distinguished himself as one of the commanders of Ptolemy I; hence he is called a prince of Ptolemy.

In the victory won by Ptolemy at Gaza, 312 B.C., the way was opened for Seleucus to return to Babylonia. In 9 years, he won the whole of the eastern part of Alexander's Empire. In 301 B.C. he added Syria and part of Asia Minor to his empire. The Seleucid era was from 312 – 65 B.C., when the kingdom of Syria was reduced, by Pompey, to a Roman province.

Verse 6 reports that the kings of the North (Syria) and of the South (Egypt) shall make a league together. Having been in a bloody war for several years , they agreed to terminate it in 250 B.C. by the marriage of Berenice, daughter of Ptolemy II Philadelphus, king of Egypt, 285 – 247 B.C., to Antiochus II Theos, the king of Syria, 262 – 246 B.C. The marriage was on condition that Antiochus would divorce his wife, Laodice, and her children, and this he did.

Since Berenice brought an immense fortune to her husband, it seemed that all would go well. But after a while, Antiochus recalled his former wife, Laocide, and her children; and she, fearing that he might later recall Berenice, caused him to be poisoned, and Berenice to be murdered with her son, Laodice then set her own son, Callinicus (Seleucus II), upon the throne. Antiochus I reigned from 280 to 262 B.C.

In verse 6, it says, ". . .but she shall not retain the power of the arm. . ." Berenice shall not retain the power of the Syrian throne (her posterity shall not reign over Syria). This was fulfilled, forAntiochus II left her and her infant son in Antioch, and returned to live with his divorced wife, Laodice, who was responsible for all three being killed. God's prophecies are completely fulfilled.

Berenice's brother, Ptolemy III, who had just succeeded to the Egyptian Throne, at once invaded the Seleucid realm to avenge his sister, who was murdered at Antioch. He annexed the eastern provinces to Egypt, and ravaged the coasts of Asia Minor with his navy.

In verse 7, we read, "king of the North shall deal against them, and shall prevail." This was Seleucus II, son of Laodice who suffered defeat by Ptolemy III. He not only entered into the fortress of the king of the North, but plundered Seleusia, Sosa, and Babylonia, even penetrating to the borders of India.

However, Ptolemy III could not enjoy the fruit of his great victories due to trouble in his own country (verse 9). He did take many captives back to Egypt, and the Egyptian gods which Cambysees, king of Persia, took from Egypt 300 years before (verse 8). Hence, he was called by the Egyptians 'Euergetes', which means benefactor.

Egypt and Syria fought each other back and forth for decades. In verses 10-12, Antiochus the Great was defeated by Ptolemy III of Egypt.

Then in verses 13-16, Antiochus the Great of Syria renewed his war with Egypt after 14 years, and defeated Ptolemy V. The king of the South, in verse 14, was Ptolemy V, called Epiphanes, which means Illustrious. Rome for the first time interfered to make Antiochus surrender his conquests. Not daring to disobey Rome, Antiochus made peace with Ptolemy, and gave his daughter Cleopatria to Ptolemy to be his wife. Antiochus planned to use his daughter, Cleopatria, to be a snare to Ptolemy, but instead, she helped her husband and put him on guard against her father.

In verse 20, Seleucus, the son of Antiochus the Great, sends Heliodorus to plunder the temple at Jerusalem and to make Israel to pay taxes to them. The king is poisoned and is succeeded by Antiochus Epiphanes.

Antiochus Epiphanes and his dealings with Israel are pictured in Daniel 11:21-34. He obtained his rule by flattery. Verse 21 reads this way in the King James Version: "And in his estate shall stand up a vile person, to whom they shall not give the honor of the kingdom: but he shall come in peaceably, and obtain the kingdom by flatteries."

(NLT) "The next to come to power will be a despicable man who is not in line for royal succession. He will slip in when least expected, and take over the kingdom by flattery and intrigue."

Dake records how Antiochus Epiphanes became king. "Antiochus Epiphanes was on his way from Rome when his father, Seleucus IV, died. Heliodorus, who poisoned the king, had already declared himself king, as had several others, but Antiochus came home peaceably (not in war) and using flattery obtained the kingdom.

"He flattered Eumenes, king of Pergamos, and Attahis, his brother, and got their assistance. He flattered the Romans, and sent ambassadors to court their favor, paying them tribute (taxes) which was in arrears. He flattered the Syrians, and gained their favor, and took the throne with their backing.

"Here, in the King James Version, Antiochus Epiphanes is called a vile person because he was every man's 'friend'. He resorted to the common shops and taverns, drank with the lowest characters, and sang debauched drinking songs with them. He did this to gain their votes and support. For this he was called by some 'Epiphanes, the Madman'"

Antiochus IV, called Epiphanes, the Illustrious, reigned from 175 B.C. to 163 B.C.. All of verses 21-34, refers to him. The Antichrist will also do many of the same things that Antiochus Epiphanes did. The Antichrist appears in verse 35.

Antiochus Epiphanes overthrew his competitors to the throne. He deposed Onias, the High Priest at that time, and installed Jason into that office, because Jason had given him a great sum of money. However, the agreement between Antiochus Epiphanes and Jason was broken, and Antiochus put wicked Menelaus in the position of High Priest because he offered him more money than Jason did.

By all accounts, Antiochus Epiphanes had quite a high opinion of himself. In fact, he even had a special name that he like to be called – "Theos Epiphanes" which means "God made manifest".

After becoming king, Antiochus Epiphanes laid claim on Coelesyria, Palestine and Phoenicia. This caused war to break out between the king of the South (Egypt) and Antiochus, who was the king of the North (Syria).

Verses 23-28 – After coming to an agreement with him (a leader in Israel), he (Antiochus Epiphanes, king of the North) will act deceitfully, and with only a few people, he will rise to power. When the richest provinces feel secure, he will invade them and will achieve what neither his nor his forefathers did. He will distribute plunder, loot and wealth among his followers. He will plot the overthrow of fortresses – but only for a time. With a large army, he will stir up his strength and courage against the king of the South.

Antiochus planned in various ways to prevent an invasion of his kingdom by Egypt, and strengthened the strongholds of defense on his borders, while making preparation for war on Egypt.

After much preparation, Antiochus Epiphanes finally made war on Egypt, and was victorious. Ptolemy was taken prisoner. Antiochus then had himself crowned king of Egypt (171-167 B.C.). By means of bribes, lies and deceit, he turned certain key men away from Ptolemy, and this helped him defeat Egypt.

Antiochus, after conquering Egypt, returned to his capitol city of Antioch, Syria, with the spoils of Egypt.

Verse 29 – " At the appointed time (Antiochus Epiphanes) will invade the South (second invasion in 169 B.C., when Egypt was still governed by Ptolemy VII Philometer) again, but this time the outcome will be different from what it was before. Ships of the western coastlands (literally from Chittim or i.e. Roman warships) will oppose him, and he will lose heart. Then he will turn back and vent his fury against the holy covenant. He will return and show favor to those who forsake the holy covenant."

While in Egypt, Antiochus Epiphanes heard that Jason, the High Priest, who had been deceived by him and deposed of the high priesthood, had gathered an army and marched against Jerusalem to take it from the wicked Menelaus, who was besieged in the castle.

Antiochus then came against Jerusalem and took it by storm; slew 40,000 Jews; sold many as slaves; boiled swine's flesh and sprinkled the broth in the temple and on the altar; broke into the holy of holies; took away the golden vessels and other sacred treasures; restored Menelaus to office; and made Philip, a Phrygian, governor of Judea. He also prohibited Jewish worship and consecrated the Jewish temple to Jupiter Olympius.

After taking away the Jewish sacrifices in the Jewish temple, Antiochus offered a swine upon the altar, and made the temple desolate of divine worship. All this brought about the rebellion of the Jews under the Maccabees.

What caused Antiochus Epiphanes to become outraged, and go on a murderous rampage against Jerusalem and the Jewish people?

It all began when Antiochus, after years of planning and preparation, made war against Egypt and Ptolemy VII Philometer. He defeated Ptolemy and conquered all of Egypt except Alexandria. He was marching against Alexandria and was only 7 miles away, when the Romans interfered and stopped him.

When the Romans showed up with their warships, the Roman ambassador, C. Popilius Laenas informed Antiochus that the Roman Senate wanted him to leave. The grim Roman drew a circle around Antiochus with his cane and demanded a decision before he stepped out of the circle. You can imagine, after this humiliating ejection from Egypt that Antiochus was looking to vent his fury. So he turned his rage against Jerusalem and the Jewish people. This war lasted about 4 years after which he died in a war in Persia.

The whole prophetic scene changes at verse 36 and fast forwards to a future king of the North, who will be somewhat like Antiochus Epiphanes, who will be known as the Antichrist.

Introducing the Antichrist

Daniel 11:36-37 (KJV) "And the king (Antichrist) shall do according to his will; and he shall exalt himself, and magnify himself above every god, and shall speak marvelous (unusual) things against the God of gods, and shall prosper till the indignation be accomplished: for that that is determined shall be done.

"Neither shall he regard the God of his fathers, nor the desire of women, nor regard any god: for he shall magnify himself above all."

The events described in verses 2-35 in chapter 11 have all been fulfilled. So detailed are these prophecies that critics have denied that Daniel could have written these words in the sixth century B.C. However, God is God. He is sovereign and fully capable of revealing these matters to His prophet.

In verse 36, a new individual is introduced simply as the king. The first thing we see about the coming antichrist is that "he will do as he pleases." That is, he will be an absolute dictator. Now that doesn't mean that there won't be opposition or conflict. Far from it! But it does mean that no one will be able to stop him! In the words of Revelation "the whole world was astonished and followed the beast. Men worshiped the dragon because he had given authority to the beast, and they also worshiped the beast, and asked, "Who is like the beast? Who can make war against him?"" This coming king will recognize no rule or authority either in heaven or on earth, but will exalt himself above every god, and will embody and seek to establish Satan's long held desire to "be like the Most High" (Isaiah 14:14). In doing so, he will speak out with all sorts of blasphemy against the true God.

From Where Does Antichrist Come?

Daniel saw the little horn coming out of one of the 4 divisions of the Grecian Empire (Daniel 8:8-9, 21-23). This was to be "in the latter time of their kingdom" and so it must yet be in the future, for these kingdoms still exist (Daniel 8:23). These 4 divisions are known today as Greece, Turkey, Syria, and Egypt. In Daniel 7, we have the Antichrist coming from 10 kingdoms (the Roman Empire), and if we did not have the vision of Daniel 8, we could believe that he could come from some part of the Old Roman Empire territory outside the 4 divisions of the Grecian Empire. But since we have, in Daniel 8, the narrowing down of Antichrist's coming, from 10 kingdoms to 4 of the 10, and definitely limiting his coming as from Greece, Turkey, Syria or Egypt, then we must limit his coming to one of these 4 countries.

If the Antichrist is coming from Greece, Turkey, Syria or Egypt, then it is certain that he cannot come from Italy, the Vatican, England, America, Germany, Russia, or any country of the world other than one of these four.

Antiochus Epiphanes was the third king of Syria (North). The Antichrist will also be the king of the North, or the fourth king of Syria. He will be a Syrian Jew. Daniel 11:37 gives some insight into who and what the Antichrist will be: "Neither shall he regard the God of his fathers . . ." He will not follow the Jewish teachings that his ancestors followed. ". . .nor the desire of women . . ." It appears that the Antichrist could be homosexual.   ". . . nor regard any god; for he shall magnify himself above all."

CHAPTER X

DISPENSATION OF DIVINE GOVERNMENT

This is one of the most well-defined and clearly stated periods in the Bible. It will last for 1,000 years.

Revelation 20:2-4, 7 (NLT)   "Then I saw an angel coming down from heaven with the key to the bottomless pit and a heavy chain in his hand. He seized the dragon – that old serpent, who is the devil, Satan – and bound him in chains for a thousand years. The angel threw him into the bottomless pit, which he then shut and locked so Satan could not deceive the nations anymore until the thousand years were finished. Afterward he must be released for a little while.

"Then I saw thrones, and the people sitting on them had been given the authority to judge. And I saw the souls of those who had been beheaded for their testimony about Jesus, and for proclaiming the word of God. They had not worshiped the beast or his statue, nor accepted his mark on their forehead or their hands. They all came to life again, and they reigned with Christ for a thousand years.

(v. 7) "When the thousand years were come to an end, Satan will be let out of his prison."

Following the Rapture of the saints, God's wrath is poured out in judgment upon the earth. Man's wickedness and defiance reaches a climax during the reign of Antichrist, who is revealed only after the Church is raptured.

This seven-year period of anarchy following the Rapture is also known as Daniel's seventieth week. It is the final chapter in the 70-week timetable of God's dealing with the Jews.

Daniel 9:24 (NLT) "A period of seventy sets of seven has been decreed for your people and your Holy City to finish their rebellion, to put an end to their sin, to atone for their guilt, to bring in everlasting righteousness, to confirm the prophetic vision, and to anoint the Most Holy Place."

At the end of the seven years the Antichrist gathers his forces in the Valley of Megiddo against Palestine, in anticipation of what seems certain to be his easiest victory. This is the dramatic moment when heaven opens, and as John saw it, as recorded in Revelation 19:11-16, 20 (NLT) "Then I saw heaven opened, and a white horse was standing there. Its rider was named Faithful and True, for He judges fairly and wages a righteous war. His eyes were like flames of fire, and on His head were many crowns. A name was written on Him that no one understood except Himself. He wore a robe dipped in blood, and His title was the Word of God. The armies of heaven, dressed in the finest of pure white linen, followed Him on white horses. From His mouth came a sharp sword to strike down the nations. He will rule them with an iron rod. He will release the fierce wrath of God, the Almighty, like juice flowing from a winepress. On His robe at His thigh was written this title: KING OF ALL KINGS AND LORD OF ALL LORDS."

(V.20) "And the beast was captured, and with him the false prophet who did mighty miracles on behalf of the beast – miracles that deceived all who had accepted the mark of the beast and who worshiped his statue. Both the beast and his false prophet were thrown alive into the fiery lake of burning sulfur."

The rider on the white horse in Revelation 19:11-16 is none other than the Savior, Jesus, returning to bring to completion God's plan on earth and to vanquish His enemies. At the proper time, He will return and show Himself to be the true and only sovereign, the King of kings and Lord of lords.

The beasts and the forces of wickedness had been gathering together to begin this great cosmic conflict when Jesus Himself returns. John takes only five verses to describe this earth-altering war. When Jesus arrives on the scene, the victory is sure, swift, and decisive. It is no contest!
There are people today who look at the world through rose-colored glasses, wishfully believing that things are getting better and better. These are "low information" people who are not observing and studying current events.

Things are not going to get better before Jesus returns.

Things are not going to get better before the earth has gone through the fire of judgment and felt the sword of the white horse Rider as He leads His saints to victory in the Battle of Armageddon.

After the sounds of battle have died away, and the fowls of the earth are filled with the flesh of the rebels against God, the millennial (thousand year) reign of Christ on the earth will come as a calm after a violent storm. This will be the final dispensation in God's program of dispensations.

Names Applied to this Dispensation

This term 'Millennium' as such, is not found in the Bible, but it is scriptural nevertheless. The word is derived from a combination of two Latin words: MILLE, meaning thousand, and ANNUM, meaning year. The word 'Millennium' simply means "a thousand years".

The thousand-year period is referred to six times in Revelation 20:1-10. See also Daniel 2:44-45; Isaiah 2:1-5; Zechariah 14:1-5.
There are other names associated with this final dispensation. It is called the Dispensation of the Fullness of Time in Ephesians 1:10.

It is referred to as "The Day of the Lord," or "that day" in many passages, including Isaiah

2:11-12; 13:6,9; 19:21; 24:21; 26:1; 34:8; Ezekiel 30:3; 39:22; 48:35; Hosea 2:18; Joel 2:1; 3:18; Amos 5:18; Zephaniah 1:7-8; 18; 2:2-3: Zechariah 12:1-21; 13:1; 14:1-9; Malachi 3:17; 4:5; 1 Thessalonians 5:2; 2 Thessalonians 2:1-3; 2 Peter 3:10.

In several New Testament passages, it is called "the world (age) to come". These include Matthew 12:32; Mark 10:30; Luke 20:35; Ephesians 1:21; 2:7; 3:21; Hebrews 6:5.

The Millennium is also called "the kingdom of Christ", or "the kingdom of God", or both, in Matthew 20:21; Mark 14:25; Luke 1:32-35; 19:11-15; 22:14-18, 29, 30; John 18:28-37; 1 Corinthians 15:24-28; Ephesians 5:5. Daniel uses this expression in Daniel 7:13-14.

In Matthew 3:2; 4:17; 5:3,10,19-20; 7:21; 8:11; 10:7; 13:43; 18:1-4 ; Luke 19:12-15, it is called, "the kingdom of heaven."

In Acts 3:20-21, it is called, the "time of restitution (restoration) of all things."

Whatever it is called, the period will be a time when all the glorified saints will reign with our Lord. In ages past, it has sometimes seemed that truth was "forever on the scaffold", and wrong too often "on the throne". But the millennial reign of Christ will see the curse lifted from the earth.

Purpose of the Millennium

The divine purpose of this thousand years reign of Christ on earth will be

1) to destroy all the enemies of God. "For He must reign, till He has put all enemies under His feet." (I Corinthians 15:25)

2) to build the Millennial Temple. "Even He shall build the temple of the Lord; and He shall bear the glory, and shall sit and rule upon His throne; and He shall be a priest upon His throne; and the counsel of peace shall be between them both.". (Zechariah 6:13). The word "both" refers to priesthood and kingship combined.

3) to divide the land to the twelve tribes of Israel as was promised to Abraham and his seed. "Unto thy seed have I given this land". (Genesis 15:18). See also Ezekiel 48.

4) to evangelize the nations that survive the Great Tribulation (Isaiah 2:2-4; Zechariah 8:23).

5) to establish the universal kingdom of Christ (Isaiah 9:6-7; Daniel 2:44-45).

Characteristics of the Millennium

The nation of Israel will at this time begin to realize the fullness of God's promises to their father, Abraham, and will become the leading nation of the world. For centuries the opposite has been true. Israel's sorrowful history of being the most despised and persecuted of all nations is familiar to all. But God's promises are still true. (See Deuteronomy 28).

The government will be a theocracy, as church and state are united under a single divine head, the Lord Jesus Christ. The Millennial Temple will be constructed a mile square on the site of Solomon's temple in Jerusalem. With Christ as King, it will become the seat of spiritual and civil government. David, along with the saints of all ages who have part in the first resurrection, will share in the government of the world. See Daniel 7:18-27; Hosea 3:4-5; Ezekiel 37:24-28; Micah 4:3-7; I Corinthians 15:25; 2 Timothy 2:12.

"And many people shall go and say Come ye, and let us go up to the mountain of the Lord, to the mountain of the Lord, to the house of the God of Jacob; and he will teach us of his ways, and we will walk in his paths: for out of Zion shall go forth the law, and the word of the Lord from Jerusalem" (Isaiah 2:3). See also Ezekiel 43:7.

The kingdom will be a literal, earthly kingdom with laws to govern all subjects.

The Holy Spirit will be poured out in full measure (Joel 2:28-32; Ezekiel 36:25-27).

There will be universal knowledge of the Lord. "For the earth shall be full of the knowledge of the Lord, as the waters cover the sea" (Isaiah 11:9; Zechariah 8:22-23).

Anti-poverty programs will be a thing of the past, for there will be universal prosperity. "They shall build houses, and inhabit them; and they shall plant vineyards, and eat the fruit of them. They shall not build and another inhabit; they shall not plant and another eat; . . . they shall not labor in vain, nor bring forth for trouble" (Isaiah 65:21-23). See also Micah 4:4-5.

War shall be no more, and the world shall know universal peace, for Christ shall reign. "They shall not hurt nor destroy in all my holy mountain, saith the Lord" (Isaiah 65:25). See also Isaiah 2:4; 9:6-7.

There will be a universal financial system. The nations are now hard at work on reforming our present international monetary system. They recognize the need, but don't know how to bring it about without many conferences, conflicts, compromise, etc. But what they seek for now will be a reality in the Millennium under the reign of Christ (Malachi 3:7-12). Tithing was practiced 430 years before the Law was given (Genesis 14:20; 28:22); under the Law, (Leviticus 27:30-33; Numbers 18:21); and since the Law (Matthew 23:33; 1 Corinthians 9:7-18).

In the Millennium, long life will again be the rule rather than the exception. The average life before the flood was about 900 years. This will again be the case in the Millennium, although people will still die. "There shall be no more thence an infant of days, nor an old man that hath not filled his days: for the child shall die an hundred years old; but the sinner, being an hundred years old, shall be accursed" (Isaiah 65:20). See also Zechariah 8:4.

This verse means that human life will be prolonged so that men will live as long as trees (Isaiah 65: 22) and for the entire 1,000 years , if they do not commit a sin having the death penalty, an act which will require them to be executed (verse 20; 11:2-5). Then, if they do not rebel with Satan at the end of the 1,000 years, if they have accepted Jesus Christ as their Savior, and if they were born again and consecrated to eternal righteousness, they will continue to live eternally in the New Earth (Matthew 25:46; 1 Corinthians 15:24-28; Ephesians 1:10; 2:7; 3:11; Revelation 20:7-10; 22:2).

A man in the 1,000 year reign of Christ will be considered an infant of years instead of an infant of days, and no one will die unless he is executed for crime; nobody will fail to fill out his days of maturity and long life. Even sinners will live through the entire period if they will obey the civil laws and refrain from sins that carry the death penalty. A man will be considered a mere child at the age of one hundred (verse 20).

Isaiah 65:20 speaks about sinners during the Millennium living to be one hundred. Does that mean that sinners will enter the Millennium? YES!

Finish Jennings Dake, in the Dake's Annotated Reference Bible, answers this question. "The theory that every person who enters the Millennium will be born again, and that the only sinners on earth during that time will be born in that period, is erroneous.

9 Proofs Sinners Enter Millennium

1. There is no statement in Scripture saying that all men who enter the Millennium will be righteous or born again. . . . the judgment of the nations in Matthew 25 will be to determine who is worthy of entrance into the kingdom; being born again is not stated as a qualification either here or elsewhere.

2. It has to be admitted that children will be born as sinners in the Millennium; can it not also be admitted that sinners could enter the Millennium? If God would allow people to be born in sin and live during that time, why would He kill every sinner on earth before then, permitting none to enter that period? That would be unjust and very much unlike the Lord and His plan, as revealed in Scripture.

Merely living at one time or another does not justify the death penalty; it is the breaking of death penalty laws that determines death in any period. That there will be sinners on earth during the Millennium is clear from Isaiah 65:20; Isaiah 11:3-5; Zechariah 14:16-21: Revelation 20:7-10. Thus, in the absence of statements showing that there will be sinners born within that period, it seems evident that some will enter it from a previous age.

3. The only statement in Scripture indicating the salvation of men at the second advent of Christ, concerns all Israel in Palestine (Isaiah 66:7-8; Zechariah12:10-13:1,9; Romans 11:25-29). There is no statement even saying that all the Jews still scattered throughout the world will be converted at this time, much less all the Gentiles in all parts of the earth, many of whom will not know anything about the second coming of Christ, Armageddon, the judgment of the nations, or Christ's rule in earth, until the missionary and civil rulers go out from Jerusalem to extend this government to all parts of the earth. The idea of a blanket government falling suddenly upon all men in all parts of the earth, and automatically taking over all the heathen is unscriptural; as is the idea that every

heathen will be suddenly killed by the second advent of Christ, without an opportunity to hear and know the gospel, and a privilege to accept or reject it.

4. The truth is that Christ and His armies (that is US – the raptured saints) will land in Jerusalem at His second advent and fight the battle of Armageddon on the first day of His arrival (Zechariah 14; Revelation 19:11-21). Then the nations will be gathered for judgment to determine who is worthy of death for mistreatment of Israel – not every person in every nation on earth, but those responsible in various governments who have had dealings with Israel in the last days. (Matthew 25:31-46). The resurrected saints and earthly missionaries of Israel will be sent out from Jerusalem to preach the Gospel to everyone (including sinners brought into the Millennium from the previous age), and to take over all parts of the earth until the whole is brought under the subjection of Christ (Isaiah 2:2-4; 11:9; 52:7; 66:19-21; Zechariah 8:23; 14:16-21). How fast and with what immediate success the kingdom of Christ will extend over the entire earth is not known. There may be some local wars with ignorant tribes in the interior of certain continents

where they have not heard of Jesus Christ in all their lives. These peoples will be some of the sinners entering the Millennium as such.

5. It is plainly stated in Isaiah 2:2-4, that many, when they hear of Christ and His reign in Jerusalem, will say, "Come ye, and let us go up to the mountain of the Lord, to the house of the God of Jacob; and He will teach us of His ways, and we will walk in His paths: for out of Zion will go forth the law (civil law of the government), and the word of the Lord (the Gospel) from Jerusalem. And He (the Messiah) shall judge among many nations, and shall rebuke many people."

Why would He need to judge and rebuke if all at that time are already born again and love Him enough to surrender to Him? If missionaries are right in telling us that at least a billion people in the world have never heard of the name of Jesus Christ, then it stands to reason that there will be multitudes of sinners from the present age for the millennial missionaries to convert. For this reason the Word of the Lord will go out from Jerusalem (Isaiah 2:2-4) and salvation will be offered to all men in that period (Isaiah 52:7; 66:19-21). Those who refuse to send representatives to

Jerusalem to worship Christ will have no rain (Zechariah 14:16-21). This alone implies that all who enter the Millennium will not be born again and obedient to the Lord's government.

6. From Daniel 2:44-45; 7:13-14, 18, 22-27; Revelation 11:15 and other scriptures, we learn that all kingdoms of this world will become the kingdoms of God and of Christ. No passage even hints that these kingdoms will be made up entirely of born-again people or that the new birth is the necessary qualification for continuing to live on the earth after God sets up His kingdom among men. What we do read of these kingdoms is that there will be sinners here at that time (Isaiah 65:20); men will need to be judged and rebuked (Isaiah 2:2-4; 11:3-5; Micah 4:3); kingdoms that will not submit will be destroyed (Isaiah 60:12), men will still need the gospel of salvation (Isaiah 11:9:52:7); they will still disobey (Zechariah 14:16-21); there will be enemies here to pull down (1 Corinthians 15:24-28); and that the final act of putting them down and bringing all things to the complete obedience of God will take place at the end of the 1,000 years (Revelation 20:7-10).

7. Zechariah 8:23 speaks of the heathen submitting because of hearing about God reigning in Zion when Jewish missionaries go out from Zion and Jerusalem to win them. This indicates the entrance of sinners into the Millennium from a previous age.

8. From Zechariah 14:16-21, we learn that the people who are left on earth after Armageddon, will be required to obey the government and send representatives to Jerusalem year by year – or be punished. If all these were to be born-again people, there would be no question of obedience and no threat of punishment.

9. In 1 Corinthians 15:24-28: Ephesians 1:10; Revelation 20:7-10, it is clear that there will be enemies here throughout the entire 1,000 years; so we must conclude that those at the very first of the period will be sinners who have entered the Millennium from a former age. The purpose of Christ's reign will be to put these enemies under His feet. The final conquering will take place at the end of the 1,000 years, when Satan leads a final rebellion against God, accompanied by all the sinners who have lived through the Millennium.

During the Millennium, there will be an increase of light, according to Isaiah 30:26; 60:18-22. The light of the sun will be intensified seven times, and the light of the moon will be as light as the sun today. Could this be because the atmosphere will be cleared so that the light which is actually available will shine through?

The natures of animals will be changed. No longer will there be fierce and poisonous animals to be avoided. These animals, as we know them now, will still be on earth, but their danger to man and their predatory nature will be a thing of the past. "The wolf also shall dwell with the lamb, and the leopard shall lie down with the kid; and the calf and the young lion and the fatling together; and a little child shall lead them" (Isaiah 11:6-8; 65:17-25).

The lands will once more be restored to beauty and fruitfulness. The thorns and briars which have frustrated tillers of the soil in every age since Adam, will be replaced with the fir and the myrtle tree in the millennial age. See Isaiah 32:15; 35:1-10; 55:13; Joel 3:17-21.

There will be Jewish missionaries, as the Jews at last fulfill God's original purpose as revealed to

206

Abraham, and planned for him and his seed. "Thus saith the Lord of hosts, In those days it shall come to pass, that ten men shall take hold out of all languages of the nations, even shall take hold of the skirt of him that is a Jew, saying, We will go with you" (Zechariah 8:23).

The greatest salvation and healing campaigns, the greatest outpourings of the Holy Spirit, that have ever been experienced on earth, will be led by Christ and His saints in the millennium (Zechariah 12:10; 13:1; Isaiah 35). See also Joel 32; Acts 2:16-21; Matthew 8:17.

There will be ordinary human beings on the earth, both during this period and forever. See Genesis 9:12; 13:15; 17:7, 19; Jeremiah 31:35-36; Daniel 4:3, 34.

As in all other dispensations, man will be tested in this one also. This time he is tested by the law of glorified saints, who are set to rule over him. See Psalm 2; Revelation 5:10; 11:15;20:1-10.

It would seem that with such ideal conditions, man would at last come through a dispensation without failing the test. But the human depravity shows through when Satan is loosed from the pit where he has been bound for the duration of the Millennial reign of Christ (Revelation 20:3, 7-9). Once more man shows himself to be as susceptible to the devil as was Eve in the dawn of creation. Satan succeeds in leading a rebellion against the Lord Jesus Christ, attacking the center of the divine government at Jerusalem. This brief universal revolt, the battle of Gog and Magog, is stopped with fire from God out of heaven (Revelation 20:9)

(This battle referred to in Revelation 20 is not to be confused with the Battle of Armageddon. This is a final purging out of all rebels remaining at the close of the Millennium. These are not privileged to go into the new heaven and the new earth.)

CHAPTER XI

THE NEW JERUSALEM – ETERNITY FUTURE

Beyond the Great Tribulation and the Millennial Kingdom, lies the final reality: the eternal state. There is a new world coming where God dwells among men. Even the blessings of the earthly Millennium cannot compare with the glorious eternity that awaits the children of God.   Even during the blessings of the Millennium, human sufferings were not totally eliminated. But in God's new world order, they are no more.

Revelation 21 introduces us to a whole new series of events. John begins his final vision with the familiar words "and I saw" (Revelation 21:1), reminding us again about Revelation's vision of future events. As such, the revelator records what he saw, in the vocabulary, language, and descriptive terms of his own time. What he actually means by "streets of gold" or "gates of pearl" may be beyond our wildest imagination or expectation. But that he sees a real place is obvious. He describes it as a city (Revelation 21:2). He speaks of its inhabitants in verse 24, its gates in verse 12, its size in verse 16, its foundations in verse 14, and its walls in verse 18. He describes the eternal state as a place of great activity, worship, and service to God. He also speaks of it as our eternal home, where we shall dwell forever.

While the number seven does not appear in Revelation 21 and 22, it is evident that the focus is on seven "new" things in the eternal state:

1. New Heaven (21:1)
2. New Earth (21:1)
3. New Jerusalem (21`:2)
4. New World Order (21:5)
5. New Temple (21:22)
6. New Light (21:23)
7. New Paradise (22:1-5)

We are immediately swept up into the grandeur of this brand-new world. It is beyond anything of mere human imagination. In these two chapters, we have the most detailed account in all the Bible of what heaven will be like. Here we find the redeemed of all time, living in perfect peace and harmony in a final fixed moral state in which there is no sin, no pain, no sorrow, and no death.

The terms "new heaven" and "new earth" indicate a brand new world is coming. Heaven (Greek, OURANOS) refers to the atmosphere "heavens" (clouds, etc.), not to the dwelling place of God. It is the old planet and its atmosphere that have vanished, and is replaced by a "new heaven and new earth." The heaven where God dwells is often called the "third heaven" (see 2 Corinthians 12:2) and needs no replacement. It is the place from which the New Jerusalem descends to earth.

The New Jerusalem is referred to as "a bride adorned for her husband: (21:2). Later, the chapter (verses 9-10) makes it clear that this is the Bride of the Lamb, who was first introduced in 19:7-10. She returned from heaven with Christ in 19:11-16, and ruled with Him during the Millennial Kingdom (20:4). Now she assumes a new and permanent position as the "holy city."

This time she is called both the "bride" (Greek, NUMPHEN) and "wife" (Greek, GUNE) of the Lamb (21:9). Yet she is also referred to as a city (Greek, POLIS). Robert Thomas comments, "The figure of a bride-city captures two characteristics of the New Jerusalem: God's personal relationship with His people (i.e., the Bride) and the life of the people in communion with Him (i.e., the city)." A.T. Robertson points out that her "adornment" is from the Greek word from which we derive the term "cosmetics." The same term also applies to the adornment of the foundations of the city, in 21:19-20.

In anticipation of her arrival, a "loud voice" speaks from heaven announcing that the "tabernacle of God is among men" (21:3). This is a most dramatic announcement. It indicates that God is now accessible to His people. He is no longer on the distant throne of heaven. Nor is He hidden beyond the veil in the Holy of Holies. Rather:

- God will dwell with us
- We shall be His people
- He will be our God
- God will wipe away our tears
- There shall be no more death
- There shall be no more sorrow
- There shall be no more pain

The summary statement declares, "The first things have passed away" (21:4). Then God Himself, the One on the throne, said, "Behold, I am making all things new" (21:5). This one statement summarizes what the entire postscript is all about: "new things". This is not a repair job. Nor is it a major overhaul. It is a brand-new creation. And the New Jerusalem is the apex of that creation.

In addition to telling us what will be in heaven, John also lists seven things that will not be in the eternal state:

1. Sea (21:1)
2. Death (21:4)
3. Mourning (21:4)
4. Crying (21:4)
5. Pain (21:4)
6. Curse (22:3)
7. Night (21:25)

The most dominant characteristic of the Holy City is the presence of the glory (Greek, DOXA) of God (21:11). The glory of God will be in full expression in the New Jerusalem. The "glory" symbolizes God's presence with

His people. The fact that He is there is far more significant than the dazzling description of the city itself.

The description of the city by the revelator is as follows:

1. SPLENDOR: as a stone of crystal-clear jasper (21:11). According to Pliny, it is semi-transparent. According to others, it is green transparent, perhaps like green chalcedony.
2. WALL: seventy-two yards high (216 feet) (21:17).
3. GATES: giant pearls named for the 12 tribes of Israel (vv.12,21)
4. MEASUREMENT: 1,500 mile cube (21:16).
5. CITY ITSELF: pure gold, like clear glass (21:18)
6. STREET: pure gold, like transparent glass (21:21)
   There are 12 great broadways going out of the 12 gates of the city. One of the streets is described in 22:1-2. It is not glass, but transparent gold of a kind unknown to us on earth.
7. TEMPLE: God and the Lamb are its temple (21:22)
8. LIGHT: Glory of God and the Lamb (21:23)
9. NATIONS: Those who are saved (21:24)
10. ACCESS: Gates shall never be closed (21:25)
11. ACTIVITY: no night there (21:25)

12. PURITY: no one who practices abomination and lying (21:27).

A great deal has been written about whether this language is literal or symbolic or phenomenological. In truth, it combines all these elements. The whole book of Revelation is filled with symbolic language; therefore, we cannot overlook certain obvious symbols here: Twelve gates, twelve foundations, foursquare. It is also obvious that John is attempting to describe the indescribable. Human language, though inspired, is not fully adequate to describe the glories of the heavenly city. Thus, we read of "transparent gold" and "gates of pearl."

What is clear is that John is describing a real place where the saved, and only the saved, will dwell with God forever. The unsaved are excluded from this city totally and completely. Satan and those he has deceived are all in the lake of fire, from which there is no escape.

The bottom line is emphasized again in the last verse of the chapter (Revelation 21:7). Only those whose names are written in the Lamb's book of life can live in the Holy City. This includes all of the redeemed of all time: Old Testament saints, the New Testament church, Tribulation saints, and millennial saints. Thus, we see the perfect blending of the redeemed in the Holy City, in that the twelve gates are named for the twelve tribes of Israel and the twelve foundations for the twelve apostles.

When the saints of all ages get home, there will be no separating veil; there will be no outer court beyond which we dare not come, but we shall be at home with God and the Lamb forever more. The city will have no need of created light bearers, such as sun and moon, though they will shine for the benefit of the natural peoples, who bring their glory and honor into the city.

The glory of God will be the light of the city, everywhere displayed, and the Lamb Himself, the Lamp. The glory of God is the light, and the Lamb is the One on whom the glory is centralized.

I Corinthians 2:9-10 (NLT) "That is what the Scriptures mean when they say, 'No eye has seen, no ear has heard, and no mind has imagined what God has prepared for those who love Him.' But it was to us that God revealed these things by His Spirit. For His Spirit searches out everything and shows us God's deep secrets."

An unpolluted crystal river of the water of Life flows from the throne of God through that beautiful city. On either side of the river, there is the tree of Life. No angel will brandish a flaming sword to keep us from the tree of Life now, for all who are in that city may freely eat of that fruit, enjoying a different kind for every month of the year!

Revelation 21:3-7 (NLT) "I heard a loud shout from the throne, saying, 'Look, God's home is now among His people! He will live with them, and they will be His people. God Himself will be with them. He will wipe every tear from their eyes, and there will be no more death or sorrow or crying or pain. All these things are gone forever.'

"And the One sitting on the throne said, 'Look, I am making everything new!' And then He said to me, 'Write this down, for what I tell you is trustworthy and true.' And He also said, 'It is finished! I am the Alpha and the Omega – the Beginning and the End. To all who are thirsty, I will give freely from the springs of the water of life. All who are victorious will inherit all these blessings, and I will be their God, and they will be MY children.'"

God long ago promised that He will one day dwell in an intimate, personal, and manifest way with His people (Ezekiel 37:27; Zechariah 2:10; 8:8).

Have you ever stood outside on a clear night with a full moon? It's amazing how much you can see in that light. But all that radiance and illumination is simply reflected light. The moon has no light of its own. Sunlight reflecting off the moon's surface causes the moon to glow. So it is with those of us who have life in Jesus. One day, we will be all that we were designed to be: we will be like Jesus in character. We will be, in the fullest sense, the children of God. And we will be filled with the glory of God. But the glory that is seen in us will be a reflected glory. God Himself will illuminate us, and the

Lamb will be the light that is seen in us. Our responsibility now is to reflect the beauty of Jesus in our lives so that others can see Him..

Other Books by Al Weesner

Roaming Through Romans

A verse by verse commentary written for the ministering Bible scholar, as well as the home Bible student. Understanding and living what is written in the Book of Romans will change your life.

Vignettes

Magnificent Miracles From the Master. Is it possible to fit 50 or more years of miracles in to just one book? Maybe not, but you'll be inspired and mightily encouraged just reading this portion of the magnificent miracles Pastors Al and Bev are able to share in this book.

To the Depths and Back
Bev's marvelous sonnet of faith, printed in Roaming Though Romans, put into story form.

Other DW Books:

Direct Quotes From Jesus
by Paul LeLiberte

A complete combining of the four Gospels into a single narrative. This book may be the first harmony of the Gospels with all the words of Jesus standing out in BOLD CAPITAL LETTERS.

Positive Profiteering by DW Grant

Is it evil to make too much money? Maybe not.

Prepare to Succeed in Show Business
(or any unstable profession)
by Gary Colombo

Why do many entertainers make millions and then go broke. Practical answers in this heart felt book written for the author's show business children.

Novels:

Blind Man's Run by DW Grant

Can a poor blind child grown up to be an astronaut and president of his country? Can a child be miss-conceived?

219

The Guy in the Red Socks by Gary Colombo

A funny yet brutally honest and true autobiographical account of 45 turbulent years in the life of a talented entertainer. Live it with him as he recounts his roots in a small town near Rochester NY, life in New York City, the thrill of Broadway, and seeing the world as it comes crashing down time after time.

Children's Books:

Bellarina, Geppetto's Lost Toy by DW Grant

What happened when Pinochio grew up and left home? What was his poor old toymaking father supposed to do?

Poi and Spamlett, Island Stuffees by DW Grant

Two Island Stuffees begin searching for their island's highest god and find more than they expected.

See these titles and more at
www.dwbookstore.com

Made in the USA
Charleston, SC
17 March 2014